ENDORSEMENTS

It has been a refreshing joy to partner with Mary in our ministry. Mary is a creative artist who paints what the Holy Spirit reveals to her. She is also an author who writes what the Holy Spirit speaks to her. In other words, Mary is full and overflowing with the Holy Spirit which is quite evident in her life and in her creative works. As you read "Seven Silver Coins", you will be enlightened, inspired, and filled with hope.

Brad Tuttle, NOCO Revivalists

Mary's passionate heart for the Lord comes through in "Seven Silver Coins", as she shares her own personal stories and encounters of hope for the days we are living in.

Pastor Leslie Lowry, City Lights Church, Greeley Colorado

A fresh collection of spiritual insights, guidance, and hope for the future. All thanks to God from whom we learn truth, and to Mary for writing down what she has heard and learned. This life affirming book, "Seven Silver Coins", is brimming with hope and a refreshing spirit of celebration for all that God has done and will continue to do.

Abigail Gerber, Mariahsachin Certified Instructor

After reading "Seven Silver Coins", I have realized our world has moved so far from God's plan for humanity. I hope many will read this book to see God's glorious world vision of the New Era Mountains.

Rose Epperly, RN and Evangelist

SEVEN SILVER *Coins*

New Era Keys to the
Seven New Mountains of Influence

MARY LEONARD

Painting by Mary Leonard painting from
her *Testimonies Collection*

ARCHWAY
PUBLISHING

Archway Publishing books may be ordered through booksellers or by contacting:

Archway Publishing
1663 Liberty Drive
Bloomington, IN 47403
www.archwaypublishing.com
844-669-3957

Interior Graphics/Art Credit: Mary Leonard

Scripture quotations are from the Holy Bible, King James Version (Authorized Version). First published in 1611. Quoted from the KJV Classic Reference Bible, Copyright © 1983 by The Zondervan Corporation.

ISBN: 978-1-6657-3094-5 (sc)
ISBN: 978-1-6657-3093-8 (e)

Library of Congress Control Number: 2022917829

Print information available on the last page.

Archway Publishing rev. date: 10/06/2022

TABLE OF CONTENTS

GRATITUDE

Thanks be to God for the Holy Spirit Fire that graces the world.
Thanks be to God for Jesus.
Thanks be to God for the opportunity to speak with Him.
Thanks be to God for courage to share these intimate conversations.
Thanks be to Papa Father for blessing us with His love.
Thanks be to God for justice.
Thanks be to God for all the battles He fights for us.
Thanks be to God for His mercies and mysteries.
Thanks be to God for this book.

I hope this book blesses each reader beyond measure.

Part One

SEVEN SILVER
COINS PROPHETIC
WORD RELEASE

INTRODUCTION

$\mathcal{I}$ have seen such anxiety in the world and in my personal friendships. I felt that this Prophetic Word about the *"New Era Mountains,"* was important to release in a small publication for all to hear.

> [2] *And the* LORD *answered me, and said, Write the vision, and make it plain upon tables, that he may run that readeth it.* (Habakkuk 2:2 King James)

My posts have been removed from Facebook and I lost my following small as it was. My channels, like Rumble, are scantily seen. I have no time to build a new following to get this important message out. I know if I do publish this book, God will send it to those with eyes to see and ears to hear because it is His message not mine. My voice will not be squelched.

God's message of freedom, hope and acceleration. It is time to celebrate the amazing future God has planned for you! Now! Time to believe like never before.

We say drink before you are thirsty, but now is the time to know freedom like never before; before it arrives. As it accelerates us into frequencies and times we have never seen.

He has awakened us to all that was stolen, including His sound. I have been adding 432 frequencies to my songs. If you explore that concept, you will see the depth of the evil that has permeated our world. Yes, evil's time is over now!

In Mariahsachin, we look at the relationship between ourselves and God the Trinity. I like Kandinsky's book about Spirit where he speaks about the triangle. We explore the dimensions of point, line, moebius, time, and acceleration in paint with God.

God is talking all the time. I hope you are hearing Him too.

I sent this book to many Christians to review before I published it. The comments were: it is simultaneously simple and deep. The main comment was to read it one chapter at a time and digest it. Decern the word of God and Mary's opinions of the interpretation. Then ask God to reveal what He wants you to glean. Great advice. Don't abandon "Seven Silver Coins" the whole book builds on the same theme. Hope you read it to the end.

I am writing in a casual style for speed, so you can receive this book before it happens. We capitalize the divine and never the evil. A big "Thank you!" to my brother and my husband for editing this book so quickly.

This book is in three parts the New Prophetic Word, Previous Reinforcing Prophetic Words and Miracle Testimonies. I hope it is uplifting and encouraging.

AUGUST 15, 2022
PROPHETIC WORD

As I see the blue fog of the Lord's love engulf the globe, I can feel the future. There is such a feeling of joy, celebration and hope. A vision once again so real as if you are living it now. This is the third time I remember the same type of vision.

More than a decade ago was the first. It was a silk feathery light blue blanket of love floating over the planet and covering all the earth. The love and joy were immense with a fullness of God and an unrealized freedom. The human condition was in tune with the principles of the kingdom on earth; from shore-to-shore globally released from the sins and iniquities of the past, to true freedom, to love our Lord, a new future. Words like joy, celebration, peace and hope are heard as the Holy Spirit moves through the world on a gentle wind of revival. This will bring a new vision to all.

REVIVAL is total! Totally here! Now! The Glory Angels are sent out. Well, we know from my half a century of prophetic words, I have no understanding of now. However, it is the third vision and it feels like now. Time will tell.

We are on the threshold of a miracle. A move of God has already started in this time. He says its magnitude is such that has never been seen on earth before. Praise God!

I see in the vision: justice is served; the voting machines are destroyed, crushed underwater. Yes, hangings have happened. Rulers have been removed and much more is to come. Replaced by God. Joy, joy, joy beyond measure. I see people dancing and spinning in the air! I hear singing and music, breakthroughs happening rapidly like a volcano or earthquake, and freedom everywhere. I smell wonderful food for a grand celebration.

He says, "Slaves no more. Slaves no more." The Lord is releasing us all from bondage. From a freedom that was fake through and through. From a freedom that was declared yet not ever realized. A freedom from a spiritual realm dictator. A worldwide terrorist was inhabiting a few bad men and women at their desire for power and money.

I feel the desolation all around. I see the carnage of this terror. **"But for God!"** He said, "The giants are falling, the mountains are moving, the mountains are crumbling, the chains are breaking, enough is enough and God's love is flowing." I know the pain, yet I see the end of tyranny. He says, "Call it in." I agree with the will of God that the enemy from within is bound and subdued. The enemy is destroyed and heaven is invading earth. The Lord's kingdom is being built.

"Like at the walls of Jericho, shout and see the walls fall! Shout and know I am God. Shout and freedom will come."

"We are free. We are free. Freedom never tasted so good." That is from a song God gave me December 19, 2019. It is a "now word."

Jesus is our inheritance and we are His. He gave us great authority and we are sleeping on the job. God is awakening us to our duties as watchers and doers. God is giving us greater authority in this time of His glory. Glorious days of freedom. He has removed the barriers, taken down the giants, made rubble of the mountains and now His remnant is to build creatively His new mountains of influence.

God has renamed the mountains of influence to include Him and His will for His children.

I see heaven coming to earth. I see breakthroughs for all God's people. Today He spoke to me about the two-tiered justice system we have been subjected to for centuries. He said, "I am turning them on their heads, upside down, inside out, and DONE!" Praise the Lord!

In 2019 God replied to my question, "God, will there ever be justice?" God said, "YES! It will be like hail! Sudden, complete, swift and pinpointed. Its memory will melt away like Sodom and Gomorrah, gone. The Justice Angel has been sent. It will be two tiered like the Red Sea Exodus. My children are saved, America is saved, Israel is saved and their enemies are gone. Choose your side, the verdict is being counted and it is over." Praise the Lord.

God said, "As heaven invades earth there will be no circling back to the old normal. NO! It is gone forever! Those evil ways are not My ways. My ways are higher than man's or baal's ways. Each mountain will be new. Each will be made by My children to prosper the world. I will show great favor to My children. I have given them new authorities. I am pouring out my end times giftings on them now. As heaven invades earth it will include Me, your God in it. You are not alone. I am walking with you, Jesus is in you, and My Spirit is compelling you to see from new perspectives."

In this new vision of freedom, I received new names for the mountains of influence – Abundance, Faith, Relationships, Communication, Responsibility, Arts and Understanding. In the next chapters, I will include the new names and how they manifest, with some comments from God. Like, "Are you ready for My remnant to build with My help? Fill the lands with My glory. Build, subdue, call it in. Call in your future. Fear not, I am with you."

God wants our questions. How do I do this? He will tell you. We must incorporate God in everything. He will show us how to include Him. "Don't get caught up in the words, that is their game. Feel, know, see and hear Me, your God."

A year or so ago, I had a dream that God gave me seven beautiful, bread-plate size silver metal coins all different and rare. He spread them out like a fan of cards. I awed at them for a while. Then I started to try to use them. Next, I found out that they open and close things. They stay with me always, like a key. I realized they were keys. Then I realized that He had trained me up in all mountains.

I thought that was a cool blessing. Then I realized that these were keys to building the new mountains. Wow! I have come so far. Starting as a warrior with a sword, to holding a scepter and now

I was honored to be holding seven beautiful keys. He said, "The war is real and it is almost over. It is time to prepare for a time of no war." WOW how?

"How, God?" I hear words like: "Give thanks, gratitude, respect, honor, mercy, celebrate, praise and worship. Use your mouth to create good things for My children. Use your hands to build good things to bless and love My children. It is about My children and **the children**. Use your feet to spread the Gospel. Remember your covenant and your inheritance. Remember the word and study it. Remember My Son's sacrifice and plead His blood for all your needs," said God.

God continued, "What was will not be again. It will be so different, but I, God, will help you. Surrender to the new. Don't compare or look back. I will be good. I am good. I have released 20 million children from trafficking in the last 5 years. I have trained up strong good leaders to replace the evil ones to help you. However, it will not be like before! You will need to assume responsibility for yourself and your lineage. You will need to learn about your birthrights and personal sovereignty. Your governments will no longer be your gods or idols. You can do it! Take the reins. You will rule and reign with Jesus. Yourselves, your cities, your countries and your world will be in your hands as it should have been all along."

God, your deliverer, said, "You can walk away from the open bird cage. You can fly! Shout for joy. Sing a new song. Be of good cheer. Shoot for the stars, you might hit the moon!" Ha Ha! I feel Him laughing. He knows that last statement is one I use for 30 plus years with my students, often.

"Peace be with you and in this glorious transition, My children. Don't strive! Thrive! I have it all in My hands. Feel My love! None are missed."

Praise the Lord. Amen and Amen

Last night He downloaded the above. I wrote quickly. I realized it was like a chapter to a book. Soon I would understand it was a book. When you add the understanding of where He is taking us in the near future to the new names and explanations of the New Era Mountains of Influence it is a book.

Recently I have spent a few months working on the future mountains with Him. I gave a lecture about them in June 2022 and again in July 2022. In the next chapters, I write about the future changes I see.

FREEDOM IS HERE!

$\mathcal{I}$t is going to be so amazing. Imagine no idols and only the true God loving you. Put yourself in this new freedom. See yourself on a new mountain. How will you change it? You are not conquering it. It has been delivered to you. Make it good now. Add God to it.

First possess yourself as a sovereign being. You have all power over the enemy through Christ. Then proceed to possess your mountains one at a time. In case you did not read the last sections, your mountain is the area of influence you know and are willing to drastically change forever. For instance, I would be willing to die on the mountain of religiosity, to change it to kingdom faith. What would you like to achieve? It is your time to do it.

If you imagine making a film in the future without porn, vulgarity, frustration and ploys of evil, what would it look like? If all that comes out of your mouth is blessings and goodness, would you make a mighty film. Dream!

God gives you your destiny. You do not create your destiny! But God uses your dreams to help you achieve your destiny for His desires. He plants hope and directions in your heart, follow the good ones. Praise God.

Some people come into their destiny in childhood. For others, it is their death that changes the world. Others grow in their talents and kingdom skills and suddenly something happens that is God bringing your destiny.

We are arrogantly told to make your destiny happen. We are not in charge of that. We can only be obedient and be where God needs us to achieve His will and that puts us in place for our destiny. God creates our Destiny!

New names for the mountains of influence are Abundance, Faith, Relationships, Communication, Responsibility, Arts and Understanding.

Everything is changing. It is changing now. Suddenly it is all different. ALL Different!!!! God has been talking to me for a while about the awesome future we are moving into. Yes, to a freedom we never tasted before, nor did our ancestors. They prayed as we did, that it would come. It is no accident you are here now.

God promised that He would heal our land if we prayed and turned from our wicked ways. God saw that we had and so did generations and generations before us. He promised if you love Me and honor your parents, it will be well for 1000 generations of your lineage. The bowls of incense, intercession and prayer have worked. Don't listen to the nay-sayers or the mass media. They are spreading rumors of bad news.

My God takes what the enemy means for evil and turns it for good. You are about to see many stunning, suddenly over-the-top, amazing miracles as He keeps His word in a big way.

You were born for this very time. There are no accidents in God's plan. The new mountains of influence will change everything. We will see baal worship is gone.

We worship God! Not the government. God is in it all. We are blessed beyond measure. Blessings from praying ancestors are being realized now. Each mountain will be created from scratch. No looking to the past. The past did not work.

Remember to teach your children what you saw that didn't work. So, they will never allow it again. You were a slave. Most of you did not even know it. Favor and goodness all come from God. The new will include Him. Praise opens the door to the Throne Room and worship lets your prayers be heard. Praise God always.

As I asked God questions about the mountains, He showed me visions and explained things. Then He took me to scripture.

I am not perfect, nor am I a visionary. I am only humbly curious and in love with my Creator. We are prophetic only in part.

As we, the Holy Spirit and I, have played with paint for 50 plus years, we spent time talking about many things. This is an offshoot of that. You can ask Him questions too. My personal quote is "The answer is not as important as the question." Also "The question is more important than the answer." Artist Mary Leonard

I teach my prophetic students to write down the myriad of questions to ask, so you can figure out which one He is answering. We have many exercises to help in hearing the answer.

I asked questions like; "I see hundreds of millions of people changing or losing their jobs. How will they provide for their families." Then He spoke about a wealth transfer. I said, "I see entire industries like major league sports falling and being repurposed. Is this so?"

God answered "Yes." I ask, "Will we learn new awesome things to work on." God answered "Yes, you will be so pleased, the world will be so prosperous but free, using free will to choose Me, in My will for My glory."

It is so necessary to fulfill God's will, be obedient and remove all obstacles, pray, command, decree, declare and go to the courts of heaven. If you have angel armies, send them on specific missions. Tear down all strongholds and replace them with Holy Spirit. Keep a record of the missions. It will help you to know where to send more. When you hear bad news send your angel army to restore the situation to God's will.

When I was in a church on a healing prayer team a little less than a decade ago, I saw a demon trip an intercessor, she did not even realize it. I bound and imprisoned him and replaced it with an angel. That angel was present there for more than 5 years. One day someone said, "Why did the angel leave?" I was not sure; I did not specify a time span nor did I say go. God must have repurposed it.

To top it all off the enemy has resided in heaven for a long time before he was exiled here and has seen God's plans. The enemy tries to copy those plans before God does them. The pretenders try to make us believe the end is here now. It is not! For many decades I have been expressing my frustration that the concept of *"sitting on the couch and waiting"* for God is a ploy of the enemy. The revival is here; not the rapture.

While evil pretends to have a health plan (false). A money plan, Peter to Paul wealth transfer is not what God is talking about. Not taxes. Only God's wealth is in multiplication. His wealth is multi-faceted. Is an evil wealth a false wealth (true). It is a carrot to keep you working for them. It is all about control! And depopulation! Not the plan God has. We need to look through God's eyes and see life abundantly, now."

I asked God, "When did we lose our country?"

He replied, "It was soon after you won it." He explained, "Most heinous to our covenant with God was when America allowed the courts to over reach and rule on the Board of Education and Roe V Wade, because that action destroyed the three branches of government and broke our God given Constitution. America allowed the courts to assume authority that was not theirs to assume. The courts wanted to create more power to buy votes and control your brothers and sisters through indoctrinating education."

God said, "They destroy My creation in the womb. Pretending they were gods and could create something. They were disguising disgusting baal worship to keep My precious children from achieving their kingships on earth."

Kingships are the children of God ruling and reigning on earth as it is in heaven. The children of God must use their souls to rule both in the God's spirit realms and in physical realms. The will of God is in the hearts of His children and the scriptures. Scripture in Luke 19:40 paraphrasing says even the rocks cry out for the children of God to be heard.

In Hosea 4:6 My people are destroyed for lack of knowledge: because thou hast rejected knowledge ….

We see the children of God are not being fed the knowledge of their true identities in their churches. God has to remove so many man-made barriers to have the children of the Lord see the workings of the kingdom and their place in it. He is removing the false doctrine that a priest or leader needs to talk to God for you. You are capable of talking to and with God on your own.

Prophetic people see in part so the mirror is not totally clear. I will cover each mountain individually. Conceptually, I will continue explaining the process of finding out the information.

He has been giving me prophetic words since, I was about 6 years old. My sister had a miracle that started a charismatic movement. The prophetic was normal in my house. Both my parents flowed in the gifts and fruits.

Both My husband and I were raised in the Catholic Church in the 1950s, 60s and 70s. My husband's Catholic experience back then was so different than mine. The Holy Spirit flowed there too but not in the same way. Now we are both Charismatic Christians.

If God wants to use you, He will. Ask and you might receive.

Early in the morning or in the middle of the night is a great time to talk with God. Then you can do it anytime. I find He is particularly talkative at night. Ask a question before bed. Have a pad of paper nearby. Remember when God is active your body may be deep asleep but your mind is wide awake. Sometimes you are positive that you never slept. Yet you did. Check in with your body not your mind and see if your body seems to have just woken from a deep sleep.

God loves questions. So, ask a question before you go to sleep. In the twilight of morning listen before you move. See if He is still talking. Say, God please seal it to my soul so that I will not lose it. Thank Him for the conversation. Ask for more.

Thank you, God, Creator of the whole entire universe or cosmos for talking with me. He loves praise and worship. Honor Him. Don't take Him for granted. Say thank You often in a day like for food, sleep, conversation, His Son's sacrifice, for making your mansion. Anticipate, He always wants to communicate.

Remembering Jesus sacrifice is a conversation with Jesus and God as we take our daily communion. We are remembering the free gift of salvation and sharing the remembrance as He asked us to do.

Include the Trinity in your thoughts and in verbal conversation like the friends they are. Grumbling about life gets in the way of hearing. It is like you have a negative friend you avoid, Debby Downer. It is sometimes that way with God. He will let you work out your rebellion and give you a time-out. Attitude matters.

The next chapters are for you to ask God questions. To explore where and how you are going to fit in the bold, bright new world. One new mountain at a time. Take notes as you read and see what the God of the impossible is saying to you.

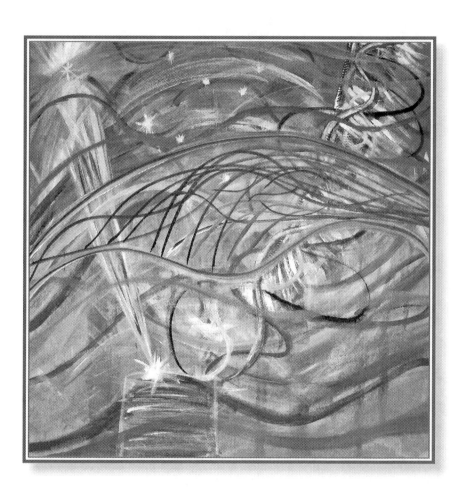

Abundance

$\mathcal{G}$od gave us grace to find a relationship with Him. We are to become a living prayer, staying in constant communication with Him. He sent His Son to heal the divide that sin created. God is all good and is a loving father. He wants the best for us all, always. As you test an inflatable paddle board before using it so it wouldn't fail you in the middle of the lake, He tests us. He tested His Son, the Redeemer. It is not His desire for us to be sorrowful. It is to proof us. Strengthen us. Prepare us for the next task.

The enemy of our soul has been wreaking havoc, causing confusion and lying to us since the Garden of Eden. He says there is a lack.

NO! There is no lack in God's kingdom. He resources all you need for your talent and good works. The love of the Lord is our provision. Ask and receive.

God spoke to me this phrase, "What do you have?" The concept is critical to understanding provision. Often, we have all we need and don't realize we have it nor do we understand how to use it.

For example, I had excellent role models in my parents. I, however, misunderstood and compared myself to them and fell short. One day I said, "God, my mother is such a great evangelist and my father spreads the glory and miracles of the Holy Spirit; I can never do that?" Before I even finished the thought, He said, "You, my precious daughter, are a pointer. Point them to me and I will do the rest. I will bring them to you." Praise the Lord. I was able to do what I needed to do with what I had.

Abundance has to do with an abundant life. Growing in the fullness of the fruits, love, joy, peace, forbearance, kindness, goodness, faithfulness, mercy, patience, long suffering, gentleness, humility, modesty and self-control. While we grow each fruit and several at the same time, we develop the muscles to do the next right thing, to learn about the next thing, so we can become what we are meant to be. If, however, we run from the process or the test, we slow the progress. Fortunately, we have an abundant community of loving, God-focused people to mentor us. Also, we have a reason why we mentor others. We learn so much when we teach. Teaching can fill our life to overflowing.

God wants us to live in the overflow. I see in the Spirit, it is a beautiful gold light that flows in a circular pattern in your head, out your solar-plexus and back in your head. This love of God and energy is always flowing when you are connected to God. It is used for His will. I see a large cup that stays constantly full for you and the extra is for others. This circle is refilled from God. If you stop the connection, the flow slows down or stops.

God is always talking to you, ALWAYS! It is your duty to connect, to open your channels to hear, see, feel, know and love the Lord. One of the most common questions I receive in my work is: "How do I open them?"

Welcome God to take control of your life. Ask for forgiveness for all known and unknown sins or iniquities. Welcome His Son and Holy Spirit into your life. Then learn how they work. A good place to learn is the manual for life, the Bible. If you have been wounded by humans around religion, remove the religious spirits from your life. I am not specifying people but the evil demonic spirits, called familiar spirits. That does not mean you are possessed. It means your heart is clouded. We live the kingdom life through our heart. Getting your heart clear is the next step in abundant living.

The next two paragraphs are prayers to facilitate abundance. Remember, it is a relationship. You don't have to use a specific prayer to do anything. God welcomes all your prayers. Yes, short, long, or even clumsy prayers are so welcome by God. I will give you two examples of prayers to help open your abundant life. Feel free to make ones up yourself.

Prayer: God, I welcome you to take control of my life and thank You for Your Son Jesus and His sacrifice to restore our relationship. Forgive me of all and any known or unknown sins. Please come and reside in me and teach me Your ways.

Prayer: I of my God-given free will, command the familiar spirit to be bound away from my life and I release or loose the Holy Spirit to flow freely through my life. I bind the love of the Lord to my soul and loosen the wounds of the enemy. All in Jesus' precious name. Amen and Amen.

It is amazing, the breakthrough and freedom that comes from these prayers. The louder you say them the better. However, it does work as a thought. The demons cannot hear your thoughts but the Lord does. It can and will be accomplished in silence, but I recommend using your mouth.

Abundance comes from the gift God gave you in the womb, creativity. That creativity comes through your mouth. The words you speak create. Speak life over your life. Call in the future. Speak life over your children and spouses. This includes life, liberty, health, character, property, wealth, family, relationships, inheritance, covenants, fruits of the Spirit, gifts of the Spirit, satisfaction, fun, vocations.

What does call in the future mean? It means say what will be before it is. Like in the time of Elijah in 1 Kings 18:43-44. Elijah kept praying even after the small cloud was seen because he knew God was on the move. He called for rain. He prophesized the rain. We see God is on the move. We want to pray into that move. That is how we call in the future.

As different as the stars in heaven and sands on the earth are the desires of a good soul. Abundance will be different for each of you. Your sister may want an acre to have a house and grow food. You may want to travel to the ends of the earth and never have a piece of land. It all starts with the relationship of Love and the communication with God.

We are in a time of transition as I write this book. It still looks very bad. Only God, can turn this around. We have heard His prophetic words and know it is almost over. The prayer bowls in heaven have tipped and He is answering them all.

I am calling it "*in now*" with many others around the world, we say God we want your will to come and be done. God, we agree with your will. We know you want only good for us. We know you are the one and only loving God. We send out our angel armies to tear down the strongholds of the enemy throughout the whole world and create your kingdom on earth. We decree it is done. Praise the Lord. We decree the glory days are here and we will build the new mountains with You. You are a God that multiplies, please multiply for us. Amen and Amen.

Abundance is about the whole life, not just business or money. Oh yes, I do believe we are in the time after the First Passover in the Old Testament where the Egyptians gave fine clothing, shoes, God's money gold and silver, to the Israelites. That is coming for us too in this "**Greatest Awakening Revival**" we are in.

As God is dividing and conquering our enemies, there will be a great loss of what was. The comfortable chains that bound us we did not even recognize. We were enslaved by data collection, by controlling jobs, and industries where we were deceived to think were not about killing humanity. The trafficking and warfare that has plagued our world for so long will be gone. We are not intended to live in this insanity.

God loves all His children, young and old. He wants them to have a fun, loving and fruitful life to multiply and subdue the earth. Oh yes, I could say go to the first chapter of the bible and quote scripture. But those who "_know_" know and the rest will find it soon enough.

Abundance touches all the other mountains. They are not standing alone. They are in a mountain range, touching and supporting each other. You can flow with them all. In my life I have been blessed to work with each of them as a business.

Be blessed beyond measure and let the overflow touch your lineage and the world. Your family's future inheritance is coming so you can steward it for the future. Beware of squandering the immense inheritance you are receiving now. Remember it is not just money, finances or business, but rather it is a full life beyond measure. Enjoy your family and build your family's mountains.

I chose the mountain of Abundance first because I felt He wanted it to be. Now I see it sets the foundation of an attitude to build on the abundant love of the Lord.

FAITH

*O*nce you have received grace and see the abundant life that God has to offer, it is easier to have faith. However, God has put a piece of Himself in you so you do not have to rely only on seeing.

Faith is not a religious spirit. Notice I did not capitalize *"religious spirit"* because it is not of God and does not deserve capitalization. The foul stench of religiosity is ending. God has only one body. The body of Christ and it is for all to enjoy the fruits of His great sacrifice and salvation. The accuser of our soul wants it divided. But the enemy has no keys, no bite, no authority. That is what the fight is about. The enemy wants everyone off the earth so God's kingdom will not come.

Foolishly, the enemy tries to steal the souls to empty heaven. The enemy wants the death of fetuses for the blood sacrifice to baal. The trafficking to worship himself. The evil is so thick it is offensive. No negotiation is okay. Some religious leaders have submitted to evil for money and to appease their parishioners and to avoid fights with governmental agencies and politicians. Many politicians have sold out their integrity for money and power. Teachers have relented for pensions, job security and ease. The movies help dull your ability to see clearly. They wear you down. The false mass media wears you down. God however wants to build you up and to protect you. You must not open doors to welcome forces which will destroy you. Rather, use your free will and choose to repel them, slam the doors, and shutter the windows!

People foolishly believe the liar and his evil promise of wealth and power which may only relinquish their promised eternity in heaven, and harm them endlessly in hell.

God wants unity in His body to serve Him by helping the widows and the orphans. Supporting each other in their walk or running their race. The body has so much resurrection power it has never used. God wants His church, the people (body) of Christ Jesus, to rule and reign with Him. The church has been awakened now. The truth of Jesus is being spread to all on earth. The truth that there is only one God with their distinct parts, the Trinity. Yes, as we are a mind/soul, body and spirit, three parts. We give Him space in our lives. We build an alter in our homes. We dedicate our homes and our children to God. We carve out time to study His ways. We take communion as a family to remember the sacrifice of Jesus to reunite us with God our Creator.

Many people in the world understand, so ask around. The truth that we have a good-good God. A loving God. That the curse of the sin of the treasonous Adam has been removed by Jesus' resurrection sacrifice and the blood is pleaded over all to cleanse and heal. The truth is that He wants to hear your praises and you worshiping Him as your God. Much else (religious practices) can become barriers to your relationship with your Creator God. The body, blood, word and remembrance of Jesus sacrifice are the core aspects of the Christian faith.

Honoring the only true God whom I call Papa Father God, Father, Friend, Protector, God, Savior, Redeemer, Trinity, Lord, Comforter and The All-in-All.

He is interested in hearing your heart and your singing voice. Seeing you express your joy and love for Him in all your ways and all your days.

Praise brings us into the Throne Room. Worship is the joy of the Lord. He loves us to celebrate the goodness He provided and pro-vides all good things. He is a good-good God and wants the best for us.

I paint in the Spirit and have been playing with Him since I was 12. He helped me design and build a house. Much like what we will be doing to build the New Era Mountains. We pray before a meal to make the food good for our bodies, and for good crops when we sow a seed. When we try a new task, we ask for His guidance, blessing and wisdom. Just as speaking blessings over water make nice crystal formations when frozen so it is with speaking blessings over your car, home and business. He wants to get involved in even finding your keys when they are lost!

So-it-will-be when we start to set the foundations for our new mountains. Do not be afraid. God is okay with "Oh, I am sorry, I did not understand." Receive His forgiveness and expect His help for learning.

Faith is not always easy, nor is life. You must always be on the alert as a watcher looking for the enemy trying to steal your faith. Rebuke the situation immediately as you feel it. Get a group of trusted friends to help keep your faith strong. Learn how to have a relationship with the Trinity. Read your bible, pray, celebrate, praise and worship.

Finally, I see celebrations all over the world with singing and dancing worshiping our God who is the one who said, "I am turning them on their heads, upside down, inside out, DONE!" He will not be mocked by the ones stealing and destroying what is His. He is saying, "I am saving America, Israel and the entire world!" This includes each of us. Praise the Lord, Amen and Amen.

In my many previously released prophetic words He spoke more about this. I will attach them as Part Two.

RELATIONSHIPS

$\mathcal{I}$ saw a vision of people at a large desk, one was an agent, perhaps a realtor or an attorney. I cannot say with any certainty what kind of agent it was. The agent was handing out contracts to sign for deeds to representatives of about ten families. The deeds were from all over the western states. The families were trading paid-off homes. They were moving to streets in a community owned by their families. Historically wounded people were reuniting and moving to live on the same streets with their blood relatives. This relocation was a huge, cumbersome task but the agent seemed well capable in completing it. There was no money exchanged. That was the dream I received.

My prophetic words come from many places: a complete download, dreams, open visions, feelings, hearing, knowing and seeing. Many times, they are intertwined. Sometimes He will take me back to an earlier vision or talks to me to append more.

Perhaps like the time where I dreamed that a friend of mine was being attacked and it felt so real and so "now", but was meant to be a warning. I warned my friend, then it happens or is postponed until a time in the future. A few years ago, an attack was actually stopped. I warned her a month before it happened, only a month. Sometimes I have waited as much as 45 years to see other messages come to pass. It is God's plan and God's timing. God is in control. My job is only to warn. Not to worry or to fret. Let go and let God.

The above dream implies to me that the prodigals are coming home. The wounded are going to reconcile. They are going to find a way to move nearer to each other but not necessarily in the same home. Again, God's timing.

God has been working with me for several years on covenants and inheritances. Both are timely and important aspects of relationships. In Moses' time five women demanded their fathers' land and God gave it to them. The concept of inheritance is important today. God gives us inheritances to steward for future generations.

We are going to learn to have a new relationship with money and resources. The root of all evil is the *love* of money, not money itself. It is how we steward money that is significant. Stewarding for future generations is an essential part of inheritance.

Finding a way to love, share and support emotionally, spiritually and physically our family and close loved ones is very important too. However, we are not to become codependent. Each of us needs to be responsible for our personal boundaries, choices and responses while loving and providing emotional support to others.

From the Abundance and Faith chapters you saw God is the focus and you must invite God into everything. Families come with gene pools of talent. My family has engineers, musicians and preachers. Your talents will be used to launch your new lives. We are here to practice for our life in heaven. I am a painter, preacher, teacher, event planner, writer, wife and mother. I spend time imagining what heaven will be like. Yes, once I was caught-up into heaven for a short while, but it was not long enough to know where I would live or what I will do either now or in eternity.

Families will be about bringing heaven to earth. Which includes having fun, spending time together, sharing life's milestones and celebrating. God loves to see us celebrate. The most fun is eating cake! Food seems to be a part of most celebrations. Even in the bible we see celebrations.

Celebrate, praise and worship God. The last time I preached, it was a "God and Country" sermon, afterwards I emphasized that eating cake was a prophetic act to show God we are in-line with His desires for us to be happy. Seeing His hand in our future.

Understand your personal sovereignty, you are the child of the Most-High-God with rights by birth. No one can remove them. When threatened or pressured to violate your sovereignty, learn your responsibility to yourself. Protect your sovereignty.

He is talking about removing (some) frustration and irritations like bioweapons, weather manipulation, evil storms, poisons in the air and food systems, being debt slaves, or indentured slaves. I believe our lives will be free to design the talents we were sent here to develop. Like being a co-creator with God, dancers and parents. All the jobs we have been dreaming about but never have the time or money to do.

I believe that as God opens our eyes to His design, we will be much more satisfied in life and sharing our lives with others. God's world is about creating and sharing.

In the time of Noah, there was a remnant of eight people. We need to secure that group of eight remnant people for our lives. This group of people will be a critical addition to your family. Your faith-based group will be the icing on your cake for celebrations. They are the ones who walked with you through your trials and tests and now are ready and able to celebrate your successes.

I see churches changing so much it is unfathomable to even write. I am not clear on the future of churches as to size or type, only that they will be unified in the gospel, praise and worship, integrated with your family and using the arenas and stadiums that were built for evil worship will be repurposed for worshiping God. Oh yes, I have suspicions, but He has not confirmed, nor even told me, so I will not include them here.

Your relationship with <u>you</u> is the most interesting part. Healthy living is changing drastically. Our daily routines (like taking nutrients, exercise and even bodily functions) are going to be very different. Faith in God to heal you totally.

I have learned so much about how the enemy has taken and destroyed our ability to absorb nutrients and use food as a medicine. God told me in about 2012 that He was bringing a revival that was bigger than Pentecost or the Red Sea.

Now we are watching many of the giants in the land fall. Big tech, mass media, big corporations, big oil, big food production conglomerates, many politicians, other nations and one-world organizations, global financial fiat money like the petrodollar, giant churches and, most importantly, big pharma. They are all going down right before our eyes.

Many idols (giants) are failing and falling. A few years ago, if I wrote this you would have thought I was crazy. Now you can clearly see it happening. You are not alone. Even many sports giants will fail. Covid did an excellent job of highlighting problems to show us a better way. God always takes what evil wants to destroy us and makes it good. Praise God!

Covid did an excellent job of pointing out that the synergy of government, media and medicine working hand-in-hand has a great impact on our health. God wants us to come to Him first. The Creator made the fruit to eat and the leaves to heal. It is necessary to have a prayer team that can pray and anoint you for healing not just secular medicine. That is part of the future healing.

With all the changes it will be so much easier to make personal routines shorter and more successful. It is truly shocking all the hidden ways that evil has been trying to destroy us. John 10:10 reminds us that the enemy of our souls comes as a thief only to steal, kill and destroy.

Have no fear, God has the plan. God always wins. God is for you. Jesus is your healer. Jesus' name is above all names and all diseases.

COMMUNICATION

Communication will change. We as a *"kind"* humanity as one, Mankind, are improving our communication skills. Over time we will use the fullness of our brains even more. I know my father could communicate over 1500 miles to me. My son says with frustration, "I can hear you praying for me 3000 plus miles away." In my wonderful husband's life, he has been frustrated by my ability to know his thoughts just before he can start to speak it. I just think it is my thought. That is the easiest way to always have the first word! Ha Ha. But it could contribute to stressful communications.

My daughter-in-love called recently and asked why so many people get the same verbiage at the same time? My answer was because when God does a move, He lets His people know. They do not realize that it is God who is talking to them. The move He is making is so great He needs everyone awake and at the ready. He is simultaneously telling the Prophets, prophetic people like me, and many others that are not even aware that He is speaking.

If you do not hear or are not obedient with a word, He gives it to someone else who will be receptive. He has many prophets in the

Old Testament. The prophets of this time do not all have exactly the same word; some are afraid of the prophetic word and are reluctant to speak; some are too fast; and some have not learned just say what needs to be said and then hold firm.

We have many false prophets who are on earth for just a little while longer. God is going to either change their hearts or remove many of them. Many completely from the planet in 24 hours, on His time schedule. I am not calling for violence. God has a plan. He will do it. He is our just avenger.

Now that we will not be collecting data on everyone and using it to promote advertising, media will change drastically. Truth matters. News will be informative and you will make the commentary and draw your own conclusions. It will not be only focused on the negative. As we spend more time in our vocations and in the family and faith areas of life, media will fade in importance and become what it should be – just a way of communicating information truthfully.

Movies and magazines will change their focus to encourage and support an honorable and healthy lifestyle to help humanity. The giants are falling so the platforms will be totally different. The "little guy" will have a voice to be heard and a space to shine. Voices will be heard!

Responsibility

God sent us from Himself for a reason. He sends us alone and takes us home alone. But we are not meant to walk this road alone. As we see, we have 8 close friends, family, marriage and the Trinity all walking with us.

We were originally supposed to govern ourselves and be accountable to the ones walking with us. Kindness was to govern us. In the early parts of the bible, we see the people were always fighting and quarreling and worshiping idols. They ended up with a government. We will see transparency in government and much smaller governments will return soon.

God is saying that the need to govern ourselves and others needs to return to the person. In a free society we need to govern ourselves. He gave us a constitution, that is by the people, for the people and of the people. Self-governance is returning. Safety and freedom come from diligently watching over yourself and loved ones. This is not for one country or another. God clearly said, "The whole world."

No removal of God will ever make you safe. Groups that were hired for riots, will disband. No more money will be coming their way. The centralized banks will not be pouring money into terrorism or treason or stimulating inflation anymore.

There is so much to say about this section. Jesus put it so simply. "Love your neighbor as yourself."

The first part of governing is knowing yourself. Loving yourself. Placing the oxygen mask in an airplane incident on yourself first. So, it is in life too.

The second part is as important as the first. We must be of service to our family, faith base, community and God to have a fulfilled life. If you miss one you are imbalanced.

Taking responsibility in the sequence of God, Self then Other is crucial to God's plan. The specific sequential order is God, you, spouse, children, others. There are so many excuses to say I am ... so I do not have time for you. Or you can do it yourself, I do not need to help, or I am too busy to care about …. We are not to be codependent but part of self-governing is opening our heart to others. It is to step up and step out. Where in the official manual for life does it say you are entitled to so much entertainment? Is your attitude about you? Are you capable of supplying your needs with overflow?

Responsibility and self-governing comes with planning, praying and discerning. I see a learning curve like a ski slope. But we can do all things with God's unfailing help. Your angel will help you too. You are given two guardian angels at conception. My angels are beautiful. They take very good care of me. Thank you, God. I have many stories about them. But this is a quick book not a long-storied book; I am sure you will read about them in some of my other works.

Your angels will help alert you to issues. Angel armies will pull down strongholds. Replacing fear with understanding.

Govern yourself, then others in the same way you would like to be treated. Kindly, but not without truth. Of all the mountains, I see this one as needing the most change and requiring much wisdom and courage to grow in personal responsibility and to reduce dependency on and dictates from big government. Ask God to share with you about the "Responsibility Mountain".

ARTS

*A*rt is a basic building block of life. Perhaps you were born to celebrate with art. For me art is the fun part of life. Perhaps you can make your calling your fun. The art of cooking, designing, music, healing, teaching, cleaning, relationships, growing and all creative industries.

Life itself is art. The art of love for your God, yourself and others. The art of balance, rhythm and rhyme. Gazing upon a sunset and sunrise without a taskmaster influencing you. The art of sipping a good bone broth first thing on a fresh new day bursting with joy and anticipation for the experiences that day will bring.

Art is baking, farming, singing, dancing and the things that bring you joy. Grow in your skills. Imagine losing track of time exploring, what? Order and reason from the heart will gently take over your life. It is going to be so worth the experience. Where do you get lost in thought? How do you like to pray? Prayer is art too. Give God glory through expressing your talents.

I paint in the Spirit as a prayer, tongue, worship and conversation. Now and the future are going to be glorious times. Don't look back except to grow in wisdom and discernment. Nothing like this time has ever been before.

Each of us should continue to explore our talents. God did not skimp on you. You have many skills and talents. If you cannot see them yet, you will with freedom and time. We are all creative by birth!

Art is a refining of our personal identity. God wants our time, treasure and talents to be focused on kingdom work. These talents you are refining are added to your Christ identity of being a child of the King of Glory making you a whole, unique person.

All mankind was created equal in God's eyes. For generations the enemy has been leading us away from our innate equality, attempting to replace it with sameness. Equality has been ours all along through our God given individuality to be our authentic self. This is the art of life.

Take a moment to think about it, we will no longer be slaves nor receive goods from slaves. We will value food in a totally different way. We will assign more value to the things we have because it will be more difficult to get new things. Recognizing your uniqueness and intrinsic value will increase the worth you feel about your new creation and yourself. You will grow in courage to create your own "art of life" regardless of the culture, temptations from the enemy or the general lack of appreciation of the true value of creative art in the marketplace.

Arts will be worth more and valued more. You invest time as a carpenter making a beautiful chair knowing it will last a long time. Fortunately, there will be fewer governmental regulations constraining innovation and creativity while lining the pockets of lawyers, bankers and politicians. Rest assured, it is the chair that will be respected, cherished and valued.

You will want to sing more often. A song sung will be the norm. Just like a caged bird expresses its joy in song as it flies from the safety of the cage to the freedom of the unknown. Similarly, as you create your art, whatever your art might be, you will begin to feel free and experience the pleasure in the joy that freedom brings.

Since I was 9 years old God has been speaking to me about worship. His desire is to have us worship and love Him. I have often preached on the horrors of baal worship in sports arenas and in concerts. The worship of man and nature over the Creator of both, is wrong focused and needs to be refocused.

Worshiping sports teams and baal worshiping concerts are going to end. These beautiful venues will be repurposed for the worship of God. Praise God! All the experience we have had worshiping a sports team will help free us to shout for joy and thanksgiving to God in the very same venues where we will celebrate the talents and creativity of our refocused sports teams and concerts.

Sound! Music is changing. The change is not yet resonating with the bands and worship teams I have spoken to about what is coming. The new sound is open, whole notes and rolling sound. Of course, you have heard rolling thunder. Lovely sound. The roar and rumbling of the lions. Women singing on the wind on God's 432 frequency. I recognize that this concept is too foreign for many to fully understand. There will be more wind instruments used. These are precursors to the freedom of sound.

God loves to start conversations with a question. God once said to me, "Mary, My love for you is so immense. I want you to sing to Me from My perspective." He wants us to sing with our roaring voices rumbling in our chest as an instrument to share the love He has for us. I do not see it as an instant change. It is coming even if it takes a while to arrive.

In my reply to Papa God I said, "You love us so much you make the sunsets and sunrises just for our pleasure. God, You sing songs over us. You save all our tears. You care about each moment of our lives. We sing back to You as we receive Your love for us. Thank You for loving us."

In the conversation He said, "I love your voices! Lovely or flawed, it's all good." Then He continued, "Why does humanity go bang, bang?" He was talking about the drums and truncation of sound. He likes the notes to fully finish before they are stopped. It is a very awesome sound. We will be experiencing this more.

It was in November 2018. I was giving a retreat for Mariahsachin students on unbridled worship. I asked God what music can we minister to you with? He said, "Your voices." I continued asking, "With a band or a CD?" He said, "Only your voices." Shock went through my skin. Fear ran through my mind. I said, "Okay!"

It went very well. Recently I spoke where there were, as often occurs, electric power and technical equipment issues. Once again, I was in a church worshiping with singing voices only. Wow! So powerful! He loves it!

In another vision I saw many flutes, each one would play a note and let it ring free. Randomly the others would too. It was beautiful.

Musicians and singers, are to be free, bold and fluid. Dancers, painters and flaggers all free to worship in a total unbridled praise to our Creator, as it should be. As it is in heaven so it is on earth. Worshiping by yourself in your home is wonderful. However, the energy multiplies and the presence of the Lord is so much stronger when we worship in a group. The larger the group, the better. I was in the Throne Room in heaven and it was larger than I could see. So, it can be here.

I was at a Walk to Emmaus event and led worshipers in a song of voices only, each person picking a word like faith, love, hosanna, hope or a sound. Each sung freely it was so beautiful. Freedom in worship.

Love is another word for worship. Art is an utterance, a tongue, a prayer, a voice that expresses your soul's love. You become a living prayer. Our soul wants to express itself. It will express itself in worship to something because we were made to worship.

In heaven we worship with our talents. We worship with sound and voice. The sound turns in to color and shape. Color like we never see on earth. It is like a painting through voice and movement, in gratitude for what God has done and is doing.

Heaven is not boring. It is filled with joy and life. God is so amazing and is deserving of all our love and gratitude. First Thessalonians 5:18 says it all. Praise God!

God has shown me so many times that our current time is not the end. There is no rapture for at least a few decades. That is a trickery of the enemy to get you complacent and lazy. Run your race.

My mother in 2009 and 2010 towards the end of her wonderful life was so sure it was time for the rapture. She would say I need to go home to heaven. I want to get off the planet and watch the soon to come return from the crystal sea in heaven. She felt you could watch things happening on earth from the crystal sea. She was ready to leave. Mother's body was failing. She died with grace and great joy to see Jesus at the gates of heaven. Once again, the idea of now is only God's in God's time.

The last Exodus was after 400 plus years of captivity. This greater Exodus is also a long time in coming. We are going into a new sound, a new era. God has never rushed His time. So, live now. Life is but a fleeting moment.

All seven mountains of influence reside in a new era mountain range. They all have similar characteristics, perhaps are even built upon the same foundation. They synergistically support each other. The sooner you learn about all the mountains, the sooner you will be at peace. Ask the Holy Spirit to guide you.

Wake up and say, "Good morning God. Papa Father God, what shall we do today?"

We will find respect for the skills and talents of others. We will respect the Creator and not the creation. We will have honor and value as individuals and not as the collective. We will respect each other.

UNDERSTANDING

"Learning will lose its walls!" The funny things He says. God loves humor!

He says, "Teach each other how to play in Godly ways. Learn to understand the Lord and how to bless your crops. When to sow, plant, grow and harvest. How to see My cosmos. Learn what it is to be fruitful and abundant. Learn the true art of communication."

How God's world works is a very interesting understanding. We learn the cycles of sow, plant, grow and harvest. We see Gods hand. We need to know in each area of our lives where we are. Like the faith revival is in the harvest stage. Your family may be in the plant stage and you might be in the grow stage. It is not a good thing to be sowing during a harvest stage.

I asked a 12-year-old without prompting, "How is God going to build the education system better than it is now?" After she thought for a long while she said, "Add God to the schools and the lessons." I smiled. What she said was the same thing I was hearing. Praise God.

As a dyslexic who struggled until 25 years old to communicate in traditional ways, I learned that communication is so much more than what we think we know. I found my voice in painting. I found that sometimes we substitute inappropriate expletives for things we can't express. I found that a *"pregnant silence"* in a conversation is okay. As I search my brain for the concept or word, life does not end. It is fine if you cannot find the thought at an instant. My brain goes so fast I sometimes need to breathe to catch up with it or even to look into space to find the word floating just right in front of me.

We will find new ways of learning, teaching, and communicating thoughts. We will be speaking freely, without the word police at schools, on platforms and in offices. We will understand that we can have different perspectives and still all be correct.

Testing in schools will not matter anymore because we will be mastering a skill or gaining knowledge, not just studying for a test. Grading will become obsolete not only because it is being used to camouflage failing schools, but rather be unnecessary because of the curiosity of the student's desire to learn more. Each student will have a personal drive to learn.

Understanding is begot by curiosity. If you don't have an interest in a subject, you don't care to learn it. Each lesson we learn in engineering, electric power or hydrology all follow the same principles and universal laws. As we teach someone canning or drawing, we use the same motor skills and observation skills. This understanding that all subjects are the same will cause a leap in understanding. That leap will propel us into areas from which we have been purposely constrained by language.

More recently in our culture, words are being redefined (or given multiple inconsistent meanings) to intentionally confuse to support cultural changes. Restoring our terminology to consistency will help us expand learning to other areas. More consistent terminology and accurate usage of terms will enable us to communicate better and to learn.

We will not be pigeonholed into the same system of learning. If you struggle, you can find a new way to learn. Learning is natural. God given.

Propaganda will be impossible because increased understanding and the expanded desire to learn will cause diverse "bottom up" educational systems to replace the current "top down" governmental focused mandates. People will find a freedom in this new way of living and learning.

Learning maybe the easiest mountain to change. Fear not, the youth will lead the way in this. Covid gave them a new zeal to self-motivate the learning process. They see and understand the issues and are just not talking due to confusion and fear. Fear is gone when God shows all of us the truth.

As I watch the parents rise up and defend their children, I have hope that there will be more parental participation in the education process. Not being slaves will mean they will have a greater say and time to devote to the family's learning.

We will be much more focused on values and character. We will learn where we end and God begins. We will see God's mighty hand move, because we are looking for it. We are expectant. We will see His mercies are new every day. When we try and fail, He will pick us up. He is a loving God.

Failing is an important part of success. You must try to walk and fall hundreds of times before you tone your muscles and tune your foot, eye and brain coordination. We don't rebuke a child for taking a long time to learn how to walk after his first few falls.

Understanding what and who you are will no longer be about the differences but about the similarities. Here too the "Walls are falling down." We will begin to learn what the words were supposed to mean like "*Kind, Mankind.*" We will retrieve our words. Our God given family of humanity.

We will learn to witness a God revealed truth to another person without the fear we feel for the pushback we will receive for being "politically incorrect" or hurting someone's feelings. We will be able to address an issue like porn or child abuse with more support. There are constant irritants that drain us now and interfere in our ability to communicate to each other. In this dark time we live in, we do not need another thing to think about. The fear, frustration and resultant lethargy that is pervasive among many people will diminish. We will be much more able to sort out our feelings and see more clearly the areas we wish to improve. We will then gain the courage and discernment to communicate boldly without fear.

We will learn how this evil self-serving, arrogant system is against us, not for us. We will see that debt slavery is the bankers trapping you into working for them in fields that did not help humanity: like pharmaceuticals and its full industry of hospitals that ensure you stay sick; manufactures of the war machine make sure there is a war to lose your children and buy their products; mouthpieces that feed you lies as truth and make sure you are censored if you dare tell the truth; agriculture and food industries that make food that retards the digestive system from absorbing nutrients into your system; and a governing system that is policy-oriented to legally enforce the whole sick plan.

If you really think about it, the colleges are gone as a place of seeking knowledge and truth. Many have become indoctrination machines to promote a political position or to institute cultural change. Unfortunately, these changes are usually anti-God and typically reflect the philosophy of atheistic secular humanism.

In opposition to these trends in our schools, God is moving and more and more of His people are beginning to reject being indoctrinated. Students are standing up and just saying "No". Parents are removing their children from many public schools or are getting politically involved at the local level to make meaningful changes in the curriculum. Homeschooling has experienced large increases.

God is eradicating porn, clarifying human sexuality, removing trafficking, restraining data collection, abolishing debt slavery, purging governmental overreach and returning us to us. It took me six months to wrap my head around the pervasive evil in our world.

Then when He showed me that the depth of evil cruelty in human trafficking was even greater than the horrendousness of abortion, I almost threw-up. As you start to see the depth of the baal worship and evil that has invaded our planet under the watchers' eyes, it will make you nauseated, too.

We must understand that people got to this condition as a result of a heinous plot by the evil one to eliminate all people from the planet. It is his way of thwarting God's plan of bringing heaven to earth through mankind, His children, whom He created to be higher than the angels, especially the evil one.

The demonic cannot create they must have people willing to manifest for them. The evil one will seduce willingly evil people using their desire for greed, power or fame to thwart God's plan to restore heaven to earth through His children. Typically, those who willingly choose evil will not repent and return to God. They are fully in the evil one's camp until death. They are the ones God revealed to me that would suddenly be removed from the planet. We will not be seeing them in heaven.

Our God is a God of mercy and forgiveness. Even those people who willingly chose to join the evil one for whatever reason can be redeemed and returned to God's favor. Repentance is the only way. Turn to Jesus and ask for forgiveness. Turn away from your evil ways.

We must understand the forgiveness that God has made available to us through Christ Jesus. Realizing that we have a loving God is the greatest understanding we can receive. God loves you and wants you to experience all the beauty and goodness He has made for you to enjoy. We will learn to love ourselves and others while celebrating our God. We will learn that we can fill heaven by spreading this good news of His love, forgiveness, and our redemption. We will understand that this "good news" is known as "The Gospel".

It is time to stop the lies that limit God. When you pray it is done. Do not negate the prayer by reversing the prayer by your own tongue. Done is done. Receive the prayer and thank God for answering your prayer. If you continue to speak about the issue as if it is still present, it will stay due to your unbelief. Ask, believe, receive, give thanks and praise God for the miracle.

Remember God promised no weapon formed against you will prosper. Used that promise regularly. Learn how the kingdom works. Stand on the word of God. Let His word flow out of your mouth regularly. Know it is your weapon. God's word, each verse, heals you.

Jesus and Holy Spirit are in you; they shine through you for others to see. When you let the word of God flow out of your mouth, whether in your bedroom or in regular conversation, you shine your light. His glory glows through you. Be the light and the salt. People will be attracted to you because they see Jesus on you. They will ask you strange questions because they know you have a straight-line connection to God.

Once I was helping a pastor with a very long prestigious history of pastoring all over the world. Everyone he meets he prays for. One day I said, "Why don't you pray for me?" He said, "You are the ambulance. I call and you run in and fix things and heal with

Resurrection Power. I know you have a direct line to source. God has you." His response meant so much to me.

I met a person a year or so ago. He said, "Mary, my mother spent her whole life teaching in the food pyramid industry. She taught it everywhere for the government. What is she going to do when she realizes, she was used to harm." I answered, "Find Jesus, see that with the simple act of asking for forgiveness for her unintended participation in evil He is faithful to forgive. She should come to peace knowing that many others were also deceived. She should then give others grace like our God gave her."

So many people will have similar concerns about their unintended participation in evil. They too are reaching for answers. Asking for help. We must reach out to them. We must awaken them to the truth and give them mercy. If we sense that evil may still be involved, we rebuke it with the authority Papa God has given us. We do not negotiate with evil!

We will learn the real meaning of the symbols that were stolen by the enemy. Then we will redeem them. We will reclaim the rainbow, the symbol of His love for humanity.

Most of all, we will learn that all the glory goes to God. Enjoy the new freedom to explore and to learn all about God's glorious world.

Amen and Amen

Part Two

PREVIOUSLY RELEASED
WORDS MENTIONED
IN PART ONE

PART TWO INTRODUCTION

$\mathcal{I}$ mentioned earlier that many of my previous prophetic words released on Facebook no longer exist on the internet. So, I included them here. These are just a few, but you will get the overall understanding from the ones I picked to include. I also have posted some on my *Painting in the Spirit Channel* on http://rumble.com/ as well as on my Mariahsachin website, easily accessed at http://www.2mea.com/.

When you read the following prophetic words, they were written as I heard God's voice. When you read them keep in mind that if the entire word is given there will be no quotes and no additional comments. If it is a dream or a vision, both God and I are talking, like in "Prophetic Word for 2016." I capitalize all pronouns referring to God or the Persons of the Godhead. For example, *Me* or *I* when they refer to God.

Thank you for reading them.

Prophetic Word
for Dec 19, 2019

In this vision I include commentary about the vision and the song that was given in the vision.

On December 19, 2019, I had a vision and a download of the upcoming election, including a song. I heard it and I got the words.

I was so excited. God wanted this song to be played for the announcement that Trump had won.

There was a navy-blue stage curtain and a Navy Band playing the song. I heard a few snare drums, bells, 12 shofars, a sound of 432 frequencies and voices that were "*singing on the wind*". I wrote the song down and called Brad Tuttle, NOCO Revivalists and said, "OK! I got a song. Now what?" It felt so urgent. The election was less than a year away. He helped me find a songwriter to get the music. I found a woman who sings on the wind but unfortunately logistics and timing squelched that opportunity.

I sent it to Lara Trump in 2020. Later, I sent it to Toby Keith. I got nowhere. Then the election was stolen. I heard God saying often, "Enough is enough"; over and over. Now I knew God would not stand for this stolen election. He would not be mocked.

On November 3rd evening God again said, "I will not be mocked!" Even though my brothers think I am crazy, I KNOW IT IS SOON TO BE OVERTURNED.

So now, I am still hopeful *Let Freedom Ring in all the Earth* will be played soon. The angel armies will be playing it.

LET FREEDOM RING IN ALL THE EARTH

© 2019 Mary Leonard and Jeff Ryan

Key of G

6/8 Intro- 6 measures on G Chord

Verse

  G

Let freedom ring in all the earth

  D D C G

Because You are Victorious… I am free… I am free

  G

Let freedom ring in all the ears

   D/G C G

You loved me so You fought my battles… … I am free

  G

My heart and soul receive the news

   Am/G C G G - D/F#

That freedom rings in all the earth we are free… … we are free…

Chorus-

Em C

 Every battle You have won

G D Em C G D

Freeing us forever God… Freedom… … Forever free

   Em C

Declare it now all over the world

G D

Freedom never tasted this good

    Em C G D

I am free… … I am free… … ->Verse -> Chorus -> Piano ‖ Am |
G/B | D | D ‖

Bridge- Am G D D Am G D

       Let freedom reign all over the earth… … because… You
are victorious

Verse 2

  G

Let freedom ring in all the earth

  D D C G

We celebrate our victory… I am free… I am free

   G

Let freedom ring in all the ears

    D/G C G

You loved me so You released me from bondage… … I am free

   G

I sing and dance to spread the news

    Am/G C G G - D/F#

That freedom rings in all the earth we are free… … we are free…

Contact us for a license or permission. Copyright 2019

Let Freedom Ring in all the Earth (Lyrics)

Key of G, 6/8 Intro- 6 measures on G Chord,

Verse

Let Freedom ring in all the earth

Because You are Victorious… I am free… I am free

Let Freedom ring in all the ears

You loved me so You fought my battles… … I am free

My heart and soul receive the news

That freedom rings in all the earth we are free… … we are free…

Chorus- Every battle You have won

Freeing us forever God… Freedom… … Forever free

Declare it now all over the world

Freedom never tasted this good

I am free… … I am free… … ->Verse -> Chorus

Let Freedom Reign all over the earth… … because… You are Victorious

Verse

Let Freedom ring in all the earth

We Celebrate Our Victory... I am free... I am free

Let Freedom ring in all the ears

You loved me so You released me from bondage... ... I am free

I sing and dance to spread the news

That freedom rings in all the earth we are free... ... we are free...

https://rumble.com/vi7cpn-brace-for-impact-june-prophetic-word.html

Prophetic Word for June 2021

God is talking here. It is the full word.

*D*ear Child,

I love you. Have no worry or anxiety. I am turning ALL to good. I told you 8 years ago I am destroying the pharmaceuticals. I am asking you to come to Me first. I am replacing them with light. Healing in Jesus is my heart and will. This revival has started. Be of good cheer, hope and joy.

I need you to understand the depths of my love for you. I am enlisting you into my healing army. This revival is not the rapture. It is the start of multiple decades of joy and freedom. I am prospering the world. But I need people right now to hold the hands of the shocked. Are you awake? Do you have eyes to see and ears to hear? Are you aware of the depths of sweeping I have been doing? Many are not.

The evil one has been lying to you for so long; it will hurt to see the depth of the icebergs when they flip. The 7 waves of pain and shock will hurt on impact. But relief is just behind and then pleasure. It is My hope that you who are awake and can see the incoming waves to help others come through this knowing it is good. Hold their hands and see Me!

The evil one has been destroying the 7 mountains for centuries. I the Lord have had enough. You have repented and My ears have heard your cries. The bowls have tipped. It has been 5 years of cleaning up the mess. Many have not seen it. Many are asleep and don't know my love. Share boldly! Now is the time to look through My eyes and see the healing of earth I am doing.

There will be 7 waves of understanding to hit the world like a tsunami. Many are anxious now not due to the bio weapon used against you, but because you are anticipating MY HAND. If you know My love you will see and heal quickly with peace and joy. But many will need your help to see.

Like the Red Sea Revival, Pentecost and the 1770's ALL moves of God! This move of God is for your benefit. It is the GREATEST REVIVAL EVER! I have been moving in all areas. But you're not getting the testimonies. You are not putting the pieces you see together. Awaken my children. Awaken now!!!! Incoming is here!

The Marxists have been plotting to remove Me from you. Only you can do that. Hold on to your faith and spread it widely.

Look and see. Freedom is here to heal Family, Religion, Government, Business, Education, Arts and Entertainment, and Media. Take this opportunity to hear and see for yourself. Then share.

It is about the children. Heal My children. I have been releasing millions of children from trafficking this year. Abortion is coming up to change. You are fully human at conception. The eyes are open to end this murder of my children. I have been opening the hearts of children to their fathers and mothers. Turning the hearts of the children to their parents. The bioweapon of the vaccine is sterilizing your youth. Pray and I will reverse this evil plot. Reach out.

I have been removing, restoring and building your churches. The shock wave of religion can be seen as pruning to the gospel, praise and worship. All the rest is being shaken. People in leadership will and have died. All evil has been and will be removed from my sanctuary. The perceived worthless who has held Me close will be utilized now. Awaken your soul. Reach out to your brothers and sisters to help them find Me.

Governments all over the world will be removed and replaced. The stealing of my authority in placing leaders is no longer tolerated. I am the Lord your God who sets your leaders in place. The dominion machines will be crushed and replaced with truth. Just as the chariots of Pharaoh were submerged in the Red Sea. In that revival I moved. The formula your leaders are using would not work. When they arrived at the sea and cried out for help, I did not say did you repent enough. When they reached the other side, they did not immediately change. I did miracles for them. There was a great move of God for His people! You will see many changes in money and the way you think of money soon. No worry it is being removed from the idol and tool it was used for. It is being restored to use for My glory.

Now, I am moving for all people. There is nowhere that will be missed, no one left behind no one but ME, GOD, will be able to take credit for it. The harvest for the kingdom will be great. I need you to enlist into My army.

Business and Education have been corrupted to the point that major upheaval will come. The tip of the iceberg has been shown but the icebergs are all going to be upturned and you will see the slime of the underbelly. It will be shocking. Prepare for impact. The indoctrination to the cult of the enemy will come forth. The devotion of the enemy will be seen. Right under your feet and in front of your eyes it was all going on. Open your eyes and ears to see the glory of the Lord in this time. Be of strong heart and know my love. Peace in the Lord will come upon you. You may throw up at the realization that the evil is so deep and took hold in front of the watcher. I have allowed you to have this time of seeing so it need not happen again.

Arts and Entertainment will lose most of their stars. The new and strong will be wonderful. You will see Me in the tails of the future. Media will be completely replaced. The schemes of the media have kept you deaf and blind. The corruption has stolen my authority. It has attempted to replace Me with an elite of evil. To remove any hint of God in your schools, family and all aspects of life. Their time has come and you will see justice in your time. They tried to steal your inheritance. I will not allow that. You will once again see Me in all your life. Your inheritance will be restored, Jesus is your inheritance, the land is your inheritance and freedom is your inheritance.

The world will prosper. The icebergs are melting. It will happen all at once. Suddenly!

It is time to see the glory of God. Look for it. Give your testimonies.

As in the earlier revivals, I will turn the hearts to Me. I will heal and release the prisoners. Freedom and justice will be worldwide. Keep My light within you! Be blessed beyond measure.

I love you so very much.

Papa Father God

Prophetic Word for 2022

$\mathcal{I}$ love you God. What would you like us to hear?

He mentioned a few of the few previous words. I reviewed them. They can be found on my blog http://www.2mea.com/ This is a list of the ones He mentioned during the long download.

- • I will destroy the pharmaceuticals
- • This will be the greatest revival in history
- • Freedom never tasted so good (song)
- • Awaken – their fires are lit; see how deep the dark is
- • See the divide and unity in all
- • Brace for impact – Join my Army
- • Today's word - call what is not yet in as if it is, purification, possess oneself and possess the new mountains.

Downloads Dec 30, 2021 through Jan 2, 2022 to Mary Leonard

Rumble link to copy:
http://rumble.com/embed/vpbp9m/?pub=bv85p

Call in What Is Not Yet

God is talking here. It is the full word.

My children I love you so very much.

My children receive. I am restoring so much this year. It is your time to receive for you and the kingdom of heaven on earth. Chin up, look up, it is well. All is on time for My plan.

Last year's sweeping went well. The evil was deep, thick and treacherous. Right under the watchers' eyes. The purification is coming and then the in-filling of the revival Spirit. The demons are leaving the home and the homeland. Fill your world with the fruits of the Spirit. Joy, peace, love to the brim. Leave no room for the enemy to return.

Drink and eat My word and My love. My provision will overwhelm you. Just say thank you. Just say thank you!

Surrender! I am with you. Now is the time to speak in what is not yet. You know my will. I am for you not against you. I am all good; not a destroyer. I respect your personal sovereignty. You are a nation with freedom, liberty, beliefs, rights and boundaries. I have removed the seven mountains from the evil forces that were controlling them. You must possess them now. Like in Joshua's time, ask and I will show you how. You the faithful must fill the mountains. First, take you. Second, take your mountains. Rebuild the mountains with your creativity, love and for mankind. Your inheritance is here now for your lineage.

Purification looks like freedom from the confinements of lies, walls, misconceptions, built in you through lies. Real freedom will look very foreign to you. Ask Me for clarification and direction. Fear not, it is good for a long while. Peace and harmony are here. Call in what is my will even if you can't see it yet. It is time to possess your land. America is covenant to Me. I am saving America. Don't agree with those who don't know Me. I am your God maker of your leaders. I have chosen and I will not be mocked. My Cyrus is the chosen leader.

Israel is expanding. I am multiplying all this year. Be expecting and grateful. I will lead you in how to share for the kingdom. This is repayment for the time of the locust. Praise your God. Say with your mouth what is not yet and it will be.

These real wars are ending in the beginning parts of the year. Pray for your real leaders, local and national. It is the enemy that wants you to separate the church and the state. I made you to rule and reign with me on earth. Do not agree with this lie. As I sweep out the sanctuaries, I am multiplying the faithful ones. The ones who welcome My Spirit. The ones that stand for My principles. Pray for your church leadership.

There is nothing that is untouched. I will not be returning you to the past. It will look so different. The past pains will fade from your memory like the pain of childbirth. In the joy of looking at your newborn.

Justice is coming suddenly. No one who needs to be dealt with will escape. It will happen so fast you will just need to know it is finished. Wash it from your mind and live free. Help your area of influence to see Me. Help them over the shock of the massive change. Teach them to worship Me and praise Me. Spread the gospel. All is well, I am doing a new thing and it is here My children.

Father God

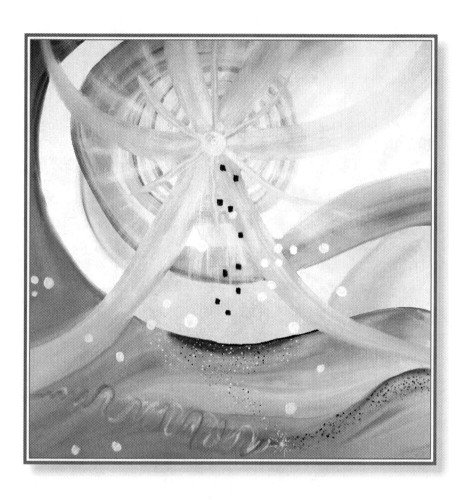

PROPHETIC WORD FOR SEPTEMBER 2016

This is a reflection and commentary of the words He gave us about the soon to come 2016 election.

My husband Larry and I, if we ask God a joint question at night and we both get an answer while sleeping, we both write it down and exchange the paper. That way we don't get the two messages intertwined in our euphoria of the answer.

It was in September 2016, we said, "What do we do about this election?" We were tired of being given 2 horrible choices. From the *"uni-parties"* as we call them. *RINO's* and *donkeys* from the party of death, all baal worshipers. God loves humor. It is funny, that the donkey is the symbol of the party of death and also it is in the bible. Knowing God's symbolism is a critical step in understanding dreams and prophetic words.

We asked, "God what are we to do? This fiery man is not our choice, we can't tell the truth about him from the lies. This woman, we call the ice queen, friend of the devil himself, is not a good choice. Are we once again left with no good choice of a leader? God, please lead us to vote for the one according to Your will. We know You are the installer of our leaders."

Then we went to bed. We both woke up at the same time. I remember the shocked look on my husband's face. We both grabbed paper and wrote our words down. I never saved the papers. I never thought they would matter to anyone else.

Larry's answer from God said, "I give you Samson." Mine said, "My Samson will tear down the five pillars and give you your Country back."

We of course were thrilled. Vote for Trump. It is God's will. We don't like to skip a vote. It is important that we do our duty. The church must be involved in implementing the Lord's will on earth. If we want to have a comment on it afterwards, we must have skin in the game. So, we vote. If all the voting members of the body of Christ would take this seriously, we would never have a bad leader again. But the churches are asleep and afraid. Therefore, we are weakened.

I thought the pillars were the three branches of government, Executive, Legislative and Judicial plus two others. Soon, I realized there was more to the number than at first sight. The number 5 means, favor and death. The pillars and Samson include the death of all in attendance many thousands of Philistines who had come to worship their dragon god, baal. I started looking more at the baal worship in our government. I started wondering how many hundreds of thousands may be dead.

Later as I was praying against this spirit and that spirit, God said, "It will be like what was meant to be in the 1960s, will be now! You are praying wrong. It is a real war, with real people dying, not just a spiritual battle! You must see the roles that China and Russia and the treasonous United States leaders are fighting and pray into that."

I asked, "Two government leaders and one church leader and many others died in the 1960s. How many will die this time?" No answer. Then, God said, "It is a rope of three strands, one rope each for China and Russia and a seven-stranded rope for the USA. The ropes of the three countries are combining together to form one mighty rope. The stronghold of the enemy is strong. Pray against it. Resist the evil one." He gave me more prayer tools and strategies to apply in the natural.

God knew I understood the cord of many strands in the bible. I had made a rope years ago when I was a Youth Pastor in our church for Sunday school class. *"Three Strands Strong."* The children tried to break it; the rope nearly broke them! What a fun lesson. Now, I was really understanding the lesson I was teaching.

After understanding the parable of the ropes, I started to see the columns. I posted a comment about the ropes and columns on Facebook, immediately got a warning and my post quickly re-moved! Awesome! Not only am I nearing the target, I am on target. Praise God!

I got several more warnings on Facebook and other social media postings. I stopped using Facebook; I closed my account. I now understand. Praise God.

My initial concerns about Trump notwithstanding, I now under-stand that he was placed in this covenant country to eradicate the new pillars of geopolitical and societal influencers.

I think now you might be wondering which pillars God began to remove through President Trump. Central banking systems, the untruthful and biased media and the power players in DC, London, and the Vatican, among others.

Well yes, I know that as I write this book, the eradication is not nearly complete. Many of my friends are not sure it will ever be complete. I know it will. God always wins. His covenant with America and Israel will prevail. Praise God.

As you start to hear God more you start to live in the future as you pray the future in. Declare and decree it is finished.

Once again, my timing often is not God's timing. Amen.

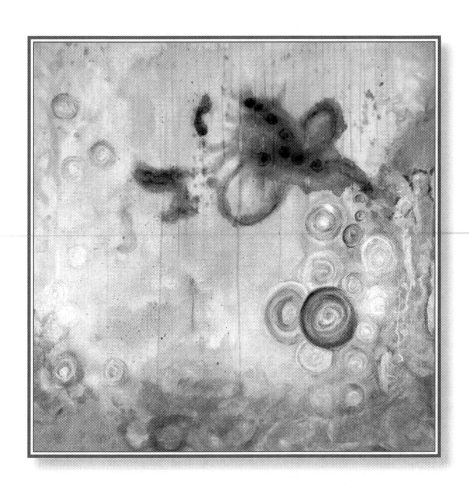

God's Love Song's Eight Week Class

*G*od's Love Song
Home Church Series from Mariahsachin Practice
by Mary Leonard

Replays are on http://rumble.com
Mariahsachin Channel - Painting in the Spirit
God is talking here. It is the full word.

Dear Child,

I love you so very much.

You are the sparkle in My eye.

I want to return you to the way I made you.

Will you let Me?

It is easy just ask Me.

I made no darkness in you, only salt and light.

I made you for laughter, joy and to walk in the garden with Me.

My compassion for you can change and strengthen you in all that you lack.

I planned to co-create with you from before the beginning of time.

I dreamed of you! You are perfect in My eyes.

I redeemed you through the sacrifice of My Jesus.

He took on all your burdens.

Ask Him and He will receive you and your burdens.

We will walk the garden earth; I made so many things, plants and animals for your pleasure.

I have a plan for you to have a beautiful future.

I clothed and fed the sparrow and so I will do that for you.

I heal you, teach you and sing over you each day.

I gave you good things to work on and filled you with all the resources.

I am accomplishing great work for the kingdom and you are part of My plans.

I want you to spread My love and welcome new brothers and sisters to the table of love.

My yoke is easy, as I will show you the ways of the kingdom.

My Spirit will flow in you; comfort you and others.

There are so many orphans, are you willing to fill heaven with Me?

Welcome My many gifts and be fruitful.

++++++

I love you so very much.

My love is made complete in you.

I gave you a map and a manual.

Each baby step you make is a joyous step in My eyes.

My Spirit gives you power, love and discipline.

I did not give you a spirit of fear but a sound mind.

My discipline is in love for you.

I want you to see your weakness as a sign of your destiny. I use your weaknesses to show My power not your power, to make miracles happen that are clearly of God not man.

I made the kinds for mankind to steward.

I gave you a birthright, of life, liberty and freedom, to spread My love and joy.

My Jesus is your inheritance and you are His inheritance.

He taught you to pray and He intercedes for you in My courts of heaven.

In your DNA I have planted your answers to your ancestors' prayers.

These prayers give you strategies and tools to work in the Spirit.

Your prophetic art becomes a prayer, prophecy becomes the marching orders to my angels to help these answers come forward.

You become a living prayer and fill the bowls in heaven to tipping.

I gave you eyes to see and ears to hear.

In my bible are many examples of declaring and decreeing in the heavenly realm to follow.

The Lord's Prayer to model your life from, stop and go signs in the world and universe to direct you. Your conscience is a mental stop sign.

The host of heaven rejoices in your deeds for the kingdom.

"My Greatest Ever Revival" is to awe you and your prodigals. To call forward the harvest for such a time as this.

My love is made complete in you.

++++++

I love you so much I want to have a personal relationship with you.

Today, I want you to know my love for yourself. I planted it in your heart. If you haven't found it yet, I want you to search for it. The connection to Me, your maker.

I want you to find Me in the sunset, in the woods, in the mountains, in the lakes and oceans. To see Me in the cry of a baby and the moan of a death. No longer do you have to look to others for the understanding of what I am doing or who I am. To worship Me in silence, with loud noise and active zealous movements.

I am here for you too; you are not alone. You are not forsaken. You are My child whom I love fully. You are My child whom I love fully.

I am singing over you; My angels are helping you. My Jesus saved you. Let Him in your heart, turn from sin.

Daughter and son, I know it takes courage to say I hear God. But you have that courage. I am not looking for perfection. If that were so, why do you come out of the womb so helpless? I know there is a learning curve. I make adjustments for that. Learn to say I am sorry and ask for forgiveness. Ask Me for strength and anointing to be the best I made you to be. Ask for the gifts. Just as you ask for blessings on each meal and each sleep, ask for blessings in all. When using your gifts remember it is not your power but Mine that you are using. The Glory is Mine. That is why I want to see your testimonies.

Many are needed in this revival. Would you have the courage to ask for the tools to work My fields? Not all gifts are the same. And you will not always flow the same way. Just have faith and trust in My love. Don't compare your gifts to others' gifts. Each one of you is different for a reason. Don't do it on your own. My Spirit will be with you. Have compassion for my people and act in love for them all. Be wise and kind.

Remind yourself, I love you! Breathe! Pray! Rejoice! Watch and see the amazing things that are happening. Awaken, My Child.

++++++

March is coming in like a roaring lion!

The things you will witness this month are coming for freedom, for the good of humanity.

My love for you and my people is rushing forward now.

Awaken your soul. Believe beyond measure that you are loved and all is going to be turned to good.

I have sent my angel armies with joy for the joyless and hope for the hopeless.

Trust this revival is for you. Hit your knees and welcome my Spirit and your personal revival. Share it. Be bold and test out your gifts.

My child, I am excited to see what you are going to do with your precious gifts.

Be alert, sweeping change is coming now. Don't miss a thing.

I love you deeply, I am with you. Be blessed. Be joyous. Be at peace and watch.

I love your praises. Don't fight My Spirit let it flow through you. I watch your praise of Me. I watch your worship. It is not in vain. You are performing for Me. Ignore the restraints of man. I love your zealous free love of My Trinity.

You My child are free.

I love you dearly,

++++++

I have come before you to set things in motion for my plans for you and I come after to help you make your dreams come true. I have left you hidden things, mysteries. Like a scavenger hunt.

Sometimes they may seem like riddles. I left numbers for you to explore. Like 111 or 3 or 5. Each means something. I wake you up at special times to talk to you. Look at the clock and take note.

My parables are veiled for you to have a never-ending pursuit for the fullness of their meaning. Words to track their roots and explore their purpose. I want you to have the curiosity and freedom to take the journey, the quest, to know Me better through the hunt.

I love you so much, that I wanted to give you such opportunities you could never get bored hunting for My nature and finding out more about Me. I love walking with you each moment and seeing your growth. I have left verses in My life manual that refer to other verses in a loop of excitement for you to play with Me, to find out what I am saying. I put verses on your heart to see what I am saying. Also, sometimes just as you are waking, I speak a verse to you so you can look for it and see how much I love you.

I like it when you get others to explore with you. When you learn to see Me more deeply, like you learn to love your friends and spouse. The same way you learn to know Me too. Come find Me and we will walk and talk together in My garden earth.

Know how much I truly love you,

++++++

I love you so very much. I celebrate you. I love to watch your celebration of the things I do for you. Whether it's a thank you to God, a dance, a painting or a call to a friend to say "I am so happy I saw God do this today."

I am preparing your beautiful mansion in heaven. Do you ever think about all the fun you are going to have in heaven with Me and the hosts and other souls? How do you imagine heaven? It is beyond your imagination; but, try anyway.

I love your hobbies and talents that you are tuning on earth. These are traits you will be using in heaven too. Enjoy the time to perfect your joys. I watch you build them for the short time you are on earth.

As you ebb and flow, I always love you. I look forward to meeting you again in heaven.

Each storm makes you and Our relationship stronger. I love it when you call on Me for strength, understanding, strategies and peace. I walk with you constantly.

I take joy in all your growth. I "Sorrow" in your pain. I cry for My people when you are in sorrow; but I know when you look up you will see Me and the correct path. I hope the birds and the flowers remind you of Me.

Celebration of the host is here for you. You will be celebrating in the streets and I will be praised for saving you. My angels are all around. Can you feel them?

I love you dearly child.

++++++

I want to hold your love in My heart. You sing to Me all your praises and worship to Me. I love to hear it so; but do you know I sing my song of love over you day and night.

I made you. I called you out of the seed to flourish. I called you to converse with Me. I called you for great works, plans and dreams. I fight your battles; I give you rest in Me. I take your worries away from you. I answer your prayers even if they stay unanswered, yet they are answered. I keep all your prayers. I count each tear and they all get attention. Sometimes you think I did not hear but I want to assure you, I did hear them all.

I am not a mean God; I don't take any pleasure in your pain. I find ways for you to get out of your mazes. To heal your wounds and also to prevent them. I love your obedience so you can avoid more pain.

I love watching you and playing with you. I love finding ways you can hear, see, know or feel Me. I love when you ask for more of our relationship. Love you and your children. I plan generation upon generational blessings for your whole family.

I love seeing your delight when you know it is Me talking to you. I love watching you discern human nature, and weighing out whether it is sin nature or human nature. I love when you clearly see the Trinity nature in you.

I look forward to each question you ask. Ask Me anything and I will answer.

With love,

Papa Father God

Part Three

SHORT VERSION TESTIMONIES

PART THREE INTRODUCTION

*G*od started to talk to me in early 2020 about the lack of knowledge of His church because people including myself were not spreading the testimonies of what He was doing. It is truly about the children!

I just thought that my testimonies were going to be shared after I was dead and my certified instructor and friend Abby, would be the one to share them with future generations. I never have thought of myself as special. One time while I was painting and writing about all the many miracles I have seen in my life and sharing them through my testimonies, I realized God has gifted me differently.

> [6] My people are destroyed for lack of knowledge: because thou hast rejected knowledge, I will also reject thee, that thou shalt be no priest to me: seeing thou hast forgotten the law of thy God, I will also forget thy children (Hosea 4:6 King James)

It is my desire to always be in the will of God and share widely as He brings people to me.

This section will be some of my testimonies, the short version. There will be no set order. Enjoy the testimonies and celebrate God's glory on earth. All the glory goes to God.

TESTIMONIES OF THE TWINS

*O*ne night in about 2007-2008, about 4 am I heard God say, "I need you to go and pray for 3 people who are dying." He showed me a picture of a couple from our church that I barely knew. I rarely store names because we are always on the move and few people are seen regularly. I may have remembered their first names in my head, but now in this writing, I do not even remember their names.

Anyway, I got up and woke up my husband and said, "I need to go to the hospital on the mainland." We lived on an island in Puget Sound. He said, "That is an hour or more away! Okay, God be with you." And went back to bed. Then I woke up our college age daughter and asked if she wanted to take the day off from the orchard work and come be a prayer warrior. She said, "No, I will pray too from here."

I went and caught the first ferry of the day to the mainland. The hospital was in Everett WA about an hour or so away. It was dark and I could not find any staff manning the buildings. Unfortunately, I did not know the name of the family. When I arrived, I put my full trust in the one who sent me, my God the Creator of the cosmos and all in it, that He would be faithful and let me know where to find the family.

I said, "God, which building, which elevator, which floor?" He let me know and I obeyed. But it was still a surprise when the father was standing at the elevator door when it opened. He fell into my arms, in torrential tears. He said, "They are dying." I said, "God sent me so I think they are not. Let us pray." He took me to his wife's room.

The door was cracked open and two doctors were there. I heard them tell the new mother "You are bleeding and you already have had two transfusions. We cannot find the location where you are bleeding." The husband and I left to go to the nursery where the twins were in incubators. The nurses said, "They are not thriving." We took the babies out and started rubbing them, praying for them and telling them, "All is well. Welcome to earth you are going to be fine. Wake up and look at all the wonders there are here." We spoke life over them for a long while and returned them to their incubators.

Then we went to pray for his wife. We repeated this for hours back and forth. About 8 am, I called the prayer team at my church. Around 10 am a prayer warrior arrived. She said, "You can go home now." My response was "When The One who sent me releases me to leave, I will." About noon, I went to a nearby grocery and purchased some roasted chicken, fruit and pastries. It was well received, especially by me and the father.

The mother stopped bleeding. The twins were accepting nour-
ishment. By 5 pm, God had changed everything. The father had
showered and was resting in the sun coming in through the west
windows, the twins were being comfortable on his warm chest,
thriving. The prayer team had left some time ago.

What a blessing to witness the thriving twins with the father bask-
ing in the sun. All was well. Praise God.

Then Papa God released me.

I called Larry, my husband, about filling their freezer with two
weeks of frozen food. Of course, he said, "Yes." Praise God for
Costco on the mainland. I left, took the ferry back to the island and
went to their home with food. I called the church community and
requested that they wait two weeks before the church crew started
visits and food rotations. Shortly thereafter the new mom and dad
changed churches. We would see them, once in a while, at the
Summer Arts Festival, until we left the island in 2017.

Papa God had saved two more of his children. All the glory goes
to God.

Praise God!

TESTIMONIES 2004 THE EAGLE

*W*e searched 20 states to see where God wanted us. In God's typical way we got on the wrong ferry and landed in a land we never even considered. It would be there. A few miles from that intersection, about 1.5 years later, we would build a house on 30 acres, with God's help.

We had just purchased the land and I was standing on the hill in an open field when to my surprise a full-grown eagle came swooping over me and brushed its feathers over my face.

The wind and shadow were awe enough, but the touch of his feathers on my cheek was exhilarating. It perched itself on a post near me and we enjoyed each other's presence for about 15 minutes.

Somehow in that experience with the eagle, I felt God's hand, it would make me feel more courageous and stronger. I would need to reflect back on that day during times ahead over those 17 years of rocky roads. I thought of it as a kiss from God welcoming me to the thin place. My own Iona. I learned much about life, God and warfare. Conquered my giants with God's help. Subdued the fear on the island and in the town. God is great, always!

This is the field where I first saw a demon possessed person, learned to bind the tongue of the enemy, I learned to rebuke an evil cloud, and learned to ask God to close the portal to the second heaven. Later I would surprise the college class when I commanded a storm to change course and in Jesus name it did. Jesus' name is above everything. EVERYTHING!!!

Testimonies 2007 The House

We took a little while to get settled and plan the raw land out. The apple orchard was already there. So, we added a few barns and lived in one for a while. I asked God to show us where the house should be. He did. We then asked for a design. It started in clay, then went to paper. We tried to hire a designer. That did not work. We decided that we could not count on the skills of the island builders to give our authority to take control of the whole project. We decided to do it one piece at a time. We gave a designer the plans and asked him to stick a roof on it. He did.

We proceeded to build it one piece at a time. Making plans and decisions one at a time as the project progressed. God was in each gentle step. Larry and I had so much fun together with God finding the perfect next steps, contractors and materials. It was a blessing to create in that evenly yoked position.

The house was exquisite in its simplicity and beauty. The best part about it was the spiritual lessons we learned, and the battles He won for us. Praise God. Truly all the glory went to God! Besides my son Eric, it is the best creation I have ever made. In both, God was the most important factor.

In that field I would hear God's voice in authority correcting me from time to time. Once He said, "Don't tell me every step of the way. Just tell me where you want to go and I can get you there. Stop telling me the minutiae, just the goal." That was a powerful lesson in getting out of my own way and trusting God. Letting worry or fear go and knowing God has it. Praise God.

He also said, "I will not help you with what you can do yourself." I learned I can help myself more than I thought. I needed to push the envelope and see what I can do on my own. While not forgetting God.

One other pivotal lesson was when I was commanding the evil to the wilderness for an eternity. God loudly and clearly, stated, "You have no authority there!" I apologized and quickly requested clarity on where my authority is. I felt like a baby learning the terrible twos boundaries. God was firm but gentle. He answered not more than Christ would. Then I rephrased the command. To bind the evil demonic one disturbing me to the desert places for 100 years, you can't come back here and you can't send your friends, I place an angel here and loose Holy Spirit to flow freely.

That has really helped me comprehend the boundaries of prayer and authority so much better. It also allowed me to try things out more, knowing God is watching and helping me stay within the boundaries.

This land had some issues and so did the land next door. That story is for congregations only.

We also did a variety of soul tie prayers. To release the soul ties of the people before us. Soul ties are not only with sexual partners that need addressed, but with land and homes also.

We had a glorious time with God in this thin place. We learned so much. The glory goes to God.

PROPHETIC WORD: AS THIN AS A DIME

*O*ne early morning I asked God, "How many shades of gray are there?"

I had gotten tired of fighting the ones who wanted me to call evil good and good evil. I have had many hard experiences and the fighter in me wants to fight. My tongue can cut deep in the fight for right. Whether I am a modern warrior like Deborah, Joan of Arc or Boudicca is no matter. That fighter needs tamed often. I learned to take up the sword of the Spirit and the Angel Armies first. My question became when should I fight and when to defer to God to avenge me?

His answer was showing me a giant golden ball. Almost filling all my visual space. He floated a microscopic dot on it. It moved from right to left and eclipsed the ball. Having studied astronomy, it reminded me of a tiny Mercury eclipsing the Sun. Then He said, "How big is the enemy? Why should it matter? Flick him away."

He took a dime and spun it. It stopped midair and stood on its edge. He said, "The gray is as thin as a dime. Either you are looking at what I am doing or you are worrying about what he is doing. No gray." No gray? POWERFUL!

The second way I have come to understand the dime parable is God can turn your life around on a dime. We must clearly both see pain and consequences to find compassion. When we feel and express the emotions, having experienced both pain and consequences, it permits us to clear our blockages and our resistance to experience compassion and healing.

TESTIMONIES 1995
FATHERS DEATH

$\mathcal{I}$ was sleeping and my father, John Britt, came to me in a dream and clearly said, "Mary, I need you to come home and help me die."

I called my sister, one of nine siblings, in the morning, I don't usually do pleasantries and none at that time. "Where is Daddy and how is he?" She answered, "He is in the Dayton hospital and he is fine." I asked, "Why is he there.?" She replied, "Oh, he had another stroke."

I said, "Well, he asked me to return home and help him die." "He can't speak," she said. "I'm on the next plane" was my reply. That was the last thing she wanted to hear!

The next morning, I saw my father. He said, "Oh! You got my message." I answered, "Yes, I did. Are you really going home to Jesus?" He replied, "Yes! Soon. I need you to write letters to all my children and have a party to say goodbye."

Reluctantly, but steadfastly, I replied, "Okay."

Since I am the most severely dyslexic of the family, I enlisted my brother Paul to assist me in this task. We prepared each letter and father approved each one. Then my father said to me, "Since you have been to heaven, you need to make me a picture of heaven like a map so I know how to get there." I did.

We called everyone to come on Sunday and had a party. Father told them, "I will be leaving the hospital tomorrow and going home to die. Most likely 3 days." He was correct. God gave us courage, peace, clarity and closure. Praise God.

Father returned home in 1995 and mother returned home in 2010.

When I look at this awesome experience of grace, I see God's hand in so many ways. I see life as one giant miracle. Here is what I experienced and felt.

1. The message got through to me, that was a miracle!
2. The peace that we had with our father's passing. We all worked together! Being the eldest of nine siblings, that was a miracle!
3. Even though mother was a mess (as she should be) praying on both sides of the situation, rebuking the enemy, asking for more years together and then asking for a smooth transition for her husband. Always saying, "God, your will be done." She was focused and went with the flow.
    God told my father he would be in heaven soon and he was. She knew this great servant of the Lord would be with God soon. His chariots arrived with great speed. He left with grace and honor to the Lord. Dad fought all his battles

relying on the victory of Jesus, including his own death, his last battle. That was a miracle!

4. When dad decided something, it was that way and done. He had closure with his ten children and showed them each that they were loved for who they were. That was a miracle!

5. There were about one thousand people at his funeral service. Fifteen priests celebrated the Mass for my father's return to heaven. As a university professor of theology and of education, he guided so many teachers to carry God's message of love and redemption to future generations.

   He was a leader in the political and cultural revolution, a committed pro-life and civil rights activist. His passion was being a revivalist. He worked with the power of the Holy Spirit to bring a touch from God and miracles in the lives of many people.

   So many miracles!

Testimonies 2010
Mother's Dream

My mother passed with incredible grace as did my father. I often tell her story. However, it was after she passed that were the times most important for me.

Just has happened with the death of my father, I was sleeping and my mother was in my dream. "Mary, I am sorry that your birth was so difficult. I am sorry your stomach was wounded and we never knew. I love you.". She had passed three weeks earlier.

Six months before my mother died, I had a gallbladder that was about to explode. It was difficult for the surgeons to retrieve it during the operation. The surgery was a success. I was sure that was my only stomach issue.

Because of my dream from my mother after her death, I once again went to the same doctor that did my gallbladder surgery. I ask him to check me out to determine if I had a second stomach issue. He did and my mother was right; my "stomach was wounded". It was suffering from a serious hernia condition. Six weeks later I was in surgery. The surgery was successful. My birth issue with my stomach was now fixed.

I am so grateful that when I told the doctor the story, he acted. God let my mother's message get through and probably saved my life and the glory goes to God.

I believe that my health issues are now finally resolved. In the process, I learned about the need to end generational curses and that this was one of them. I wanted to clear them from my family legacy forever. I believe they have been cleared. Prayer works. That was my miracle!

Testimonies 2011 Operation, 24 Hours with God

*E*ven to this day one of the most awesome times with God's presence in my life was after the operation which fixed the hernia issue with my stomach. The post-surgery hospital room in a renowned Seattle hospital was so thick with God's presence. I asked my husband to come back in 24 hours. He returned to the island where we lived and then returned 24 hours later.

The presence of God was so healing, I used no medications, kept the curtains closed, the door shut and no TV. It was a God party just for me. The nurse called me an angel. I laughed, but the nurse kept wanting me to push the self-administered pain med. I saw no reason.

Many lovely things happened, but the most important one was when God said, "You have been a good and faithful servant. You no longer need to go looking for them. I will bring them to you." He has. Praise God.

We often hear the words and then the interpretation comes later. At first, I was expecting He would bring them to my home. Later I learned that He will bring them to me where ever I am.

I just finished a 2-year long project involving hundreds of people to remove fear from a town. We created 18 sculpture gardens for a competition. I drove up and down the island, blessing the people. Releasing heaven's glory. Releasing the love of the Lord. Rebuking fear. Praise God it was very successful.

I learned so much from that time. The projects were going to get so much easier. The glory goes to God. Always.

TESTIMONIES 1961 MIRACLE

This pivotal miracle started a Charismatic Movement in the Catholic Church that still is visible. It started the "Duquesne Outpouring" and was the first miracle I saw in my short 4-year-old life. I go into great detail in my book, "The God Factor in Recovery, Mess to Miracles."

One of the thousand things I learned from that movement was that God is always good and that he turns what the enemy wants for evil to good. Praise God.

I was born again in 1961 and knew the Holy Spirit intimately. I was permanently changed. God, My Father, is an awesome friend.

It must have been thousands of miracles!

TESTIMONIES 1966 CAUGHT UP TO HEAVEN

As a child I loved worshiping Father God. My parents loved to sing Psalms and Proverbs while we did chores and before bed. My father would read us the adult classics, C.S. Lewis and scripture. He did not read us the little children's versions. They did convert children's games like Itsy Bitsy Spider into other more godly games. *V for Victory,* they would have us hold our hands up in the air like we were praising God. Father would say "V for Christ Victory." Then they would pretend they had a pitcher of Holy Spirit power and they would come to each of us and pour out the pitcher on our heads. The V for victory in Christ was now filled with His Spirit. We each became a chalice of God's Holy Spirits power. I never forgot that.

It was one of the first videos I posted on YouTube. Now it moved to Rumble.com at "Painting in the Spirit." I posted a modernized version of my parents *V for Victory* game on Rumble.

https://rumble.com/ve02lb-child-holy-spirit-experience-first-posted-in-2016.html

I was nine years old, a rowdy worshiper. I was caught-up to the Throne Room and saw worship there. There was so much amazing powerful color not seen anywhere on earth. It was so intense. Children in floating bubbles with rainbows flowing in the bubbles. I saw sound as color and shapes. The sounds were awesome, rolling thunder of joy and the sound of words like "Holy, Holy, Holy" and more. Words on words in song. Open, free sound. No beat, like on earth. I saw the three balls of light on thrones and saints and angels everywhere. Jesus said, "You will be a worship leader and a presenter of retreats."

I came back and told my father all about it.

It was two years after I was in heaven and nothing happened yet. I did not know a prophetic word could be for later. That little eleven-year-old girl was so upset. I thought my life was to work for God the Father and I had failed. I was inconsolable. I was a failure! Drama was at its peak. I can laugh now but then the sky was falling!

My parents were very persuasive. They went to the church and said, "We need you to help her." So, the priest had a separate service for me and anyone who wanted to attend. I became the youth pastor in a Catholic Church. I was in charge of the band and the music at 9:30 in the morning on Sunday in the chapel. It became a well sought-after church service even for the adults.

At 15, I was disillusioned once again, that the whole Catholic Church had not seen the light, that we needed to worship like they do in heaven. I got money together and had the opportunity to go have a personal meeting with the Pope. That experience is a whole other story for book of its own.

Testimonies 1969
Mariahsachin

My youngest sibling was born summer of 1969. Mother needed a vacation. This birth was number 10 in 12 years. We all went to Wisconsin to visit my aunt. I thought life was awesome, but did not realize the stress I was under. My aunt did. She told me, "You are in crisis." I, of course, thought I was normal. She said, "We must teach you how to paint in the Spirit so that He can help you." It was two weeks of intense focused training and so much fun. I was hooked.

I learned how to converse with Spirit in painting and to interpret the painting. The tongue of unknown things. An utterance of millions of words in each of my Mariahsachin paintings, unlike a regular painting of only a thousand words. The spiritual tongue can be sound, color or paint. Utterances of God is to edify you and others.

Your talents and gifting are born in you to be used on earth and when again you get to heaven. I began painting all night long. loving God. I would ask for a vision, a picture, a color or a shape. I loved it! Talking with God!

I sold my first painting at 13 years old to a doctor. She purchased it to hang in the Kettering Hospital in Ohio.

As I got older, I asked my aunt the name of what I was doing and she said, "*Essence*."

I asked if I could rename it to something cooler! "Yes." I researched essence and named it the "*Essence of the Essence*", "***Mariahsachin*.*"* I have been teaching it since I learned it so long ago.

Then, I started to paint in front of church and worship congregations. It edified the church, showing others that worship was part of all that we do. Some pastors want to have the Spirit flow in their church. They will periodically welcome portions of charismatic worship. Then, when they see what biblical freedom in worship really means, some of them reconsider and kick the Spirit worship out of the service. It seems to me so that they can remain in control of the service.

One night in 2013 at 3 am God said, "Write this down." I requested to wait until morning. The answer was, "No". I wrote it down. Then in the morning I asked, "God, what do you want me to do with it?" He said, "Read it to your Mariahsachin class this morning."

I typed what He downloaded and read it to my class. It was a child's book. My husband was there that day. We watched the room all in tears. I went home and said, to God, "That moved them." God said, "I want you to paint the book in front of churches along the Front Range." That took me two years to complete. Then I asked, "Now what, God?" He said, "Sell your Colorado house and publish it."

We did. The book is *God's Little Princess, A Child's Abstract Journey*. The book was published in 2015.

The book is about a little girl who paints in the Spirit from birth to death. It is a great way to start a conversation with anyone about praise and worship, painting for God and climbing the seven life mountains. The paintings are from God's perspective, using the pointer you travel into the painting and see your path and moment. It opens many interesting conversations to explore God in your life.

As a praise painter, I have been in hundreds of services in many different denominations and seen the difference in churches. Some pastors are great coming well prepared and then letting God rewrite the sermon and take over the service. I like when the Holy Spirit takes over the worship to the point there is no message. I like when Spirit flows and they have to go an hour or two longer. I like when Holy Spirit comes and it is days later and you are still at church praising. The best is 24-hour watcher prayer at a church.

TESTIMONIES, PROPHETIC WORD FOR CHURCHES

I picked these two churches as examples to show how God works.

The Rock Church, Castle Rock, Colorado

We attended the Rock Church from 2011 through 2015. I had many prophetic words for them and it was a wonderful time teaching Mariahsachin Style Painting, "Painting in the Spirit".

On this one day I was listening to the message. I kept thinking that this message was wonderful interview for the Senior Assistant Pastors position.

Well, I had not heard yet that the position was retiring. I had not been told this was in reality an interview. In my normal unfiltered way; without any thought; as we were shaking the pastor's hand on the way out; I blurted out, "Nice interview. I would hire him for the Senior Assistant Pastors position." Shock was on the Pastor's face. His color drained. Then he said, "Say that again." So, I did.

It turned out that the man currently holding the position was planning to retire and was wrestling with how to tell the church. That day the current Senior Assistant Pastor and the Pastor talked and started an exit/transition plan for the Senior Assistant Pastor.

It is not uncommon for me to give prophetic words without even knowing it.

Carr Community Church, Hub of Revival Colorado

I was scheduled on July 3, 2022 to give the "God and Country Message" to Carr Community Church.

On June 11, 2022 I sat down to prepare my message and asked God to give me a word for the congregation or for the community as a whole. Then I wrote what I heard. It was a powerful word. I needed confirmation that I heard it correctly. As a substitute preacher, who had never attended the church before for a Sunday service. I went to a Sunday service on June 19 at their church. That Sunday I attended and saw that they were ready for such a powerful word. Praise God.

The following Sunday, June 26, I scheduled time with a pastor friend, Howard Skinner, to rehearse the message and get additional confirmation. This could be another chapter in itself.

When we arrived, Pastor Howard said, "I know your word is good, give it to them. We have a change of plans for today. Please pray with me. I am 93 years old and God has finished my race. We need to call the chariots!"

My husband and I were shocked it was his time. Howard had many miracles that year alone and was not in failing health. He was tired and his mission was complete. He had walked alongside and inspired many people of great faith who passed to heaven with great grace and honor.

A little over a year earlier Howard asked my husband and I to walk him to death. I thought it would be a long while. After a long comprehensive discussion with Pastor Howard, we were honored to call in his chariots. We asked Jesus to join the team escorting Howard personally home, due to his 70 years of service preaching for the Lord.

God, quickly honored Howard's request, Pastor Howard Skinner went to his reward on July 20th 2022.

His confirmation to me of the mighty word was received. The message went very well when I gave it on July 3, 2022. The congregation received it with shofar horns and some standing and clapping. Praise God.

It is important to confirm some words with other servants of the Lord to insure you are hearing it correctly. It has been my pleasure and honor to be a part of a worldwide community of others who hear our Creator's voice. This is the word I gave Carr Community Church on July 3, 2022 in my *God and Country Message.*

The Word I Received for Carr Community Church June 11

God sees your love for Him.

He wants you to see freedom from the debt slavery your world has been in.

He wants you to take your part in building the seven mountains for the "New ERA."

God sees you welcoming His revival that is happening here.

No evil can enter this property, and will flee from this area.

No form of baal worship will be tolerated here.

Your church is anointed:

To gather the lost and share the hope and love of the Lord,

To soak in the presence of the Lord Jesus,

To break-through the evil using your full authority given to you through Christ,

To maintain your soul as sovereign beings,

To be free from birth as God made you,

To claim the future,

To claim your rights, life, liberty and property as a covenant member of the republic.

To engage in full loving worship of God, the Trinity and Jesus will be free to flow and fill the hearts of the community and others.

At the last second, I felt God wanted to post a Glory Angel on the roof to light the way for revival. I posted one there. I know God can move or replace it at any time but for then it was shining like a beacon!

Praise The Lord, Amen and Amen.

MY ANGELS

I have seen my angels in action. I have seen them save me and my friend Connie in the mountains, when a car's engine just in front of us blew up. I have seen my angel watching me paint through my spiritual eyes. I have seen the demonic. I have watched my angels flash at me. I have seen them in my dreams.

One day, I had an angel manifest to save me from great harm. My mother had a stroke. I was being dropped off in a very rough neighborhood. I was unaware that the hospital parking lots had become a killing ground. A place you could be stabbed for no reason, robbed and killed.

My loving awesome husband had no idea either. We saw a door near the parking garage and falsely assumed I could enter there. He dropped me off. The door was locked and for employee cards opening only. I was crying and walking, not knowing I was heading right for a drug deal going down in this notoriously dangerous area.

All of the sudden there was a very large man in both height and stature, an extremely dark-skinned man who appeared beside me.

I could feel the presence of the Lord. It did not frighten me. It was an angel or my angel. I did not ask. I awakened from my pain to see the danger. He said sternly, "You are in the wrong place!" That was the end of the conversation. He walked me the two blocks to the correct door, crossing to the other side of the road to avoid the drug deal situation. He took me to the correct door and then vanished in thin air.

Praise God for His endless protection. He fights our battles for us. The glory goes to Him.

How do I receive
Jesus In My Heart

$\mathcal{P}$eople say do you know Jesus? Have you been saved? My mother's favorite, "Have you received the free gift of eternal life and grace?" Do you want to be free? Have you welcomed love into your heart? Do you want to surrender and give shame and guilt and self-abuse away? Are you a sheep or a goat? Where will you spend eternity?

These questions are all the same question. Different ways of welcoming you into the family. A way of showing God's love and light to you. A way of welcoming you into the family of God, Jesus and Holy Spirit. Joining with a brother and sisterhood of orphans, now family. Jesus made simple.

When some one reaches out to you in one of these ways they are not shaming or guilting you. They are saying you are welcome into the family of Christ.

Jesus is so in love with you! He is chasing you in the Spiritual Realm. If you let Him catch you, you will find peace and forgiveness that you long for. You are no different than the rest of us. It is written on our souls from when we were created. That is why you know in your heart; it should not be this hard.

Once you meet Him you will know it. There are different ways of expressing that you have received Jesus in your heart. Some say:

I am a believer that means I know Jesus
I welcomed Him into my heart and my life
I surrendered my ways of trying, to live life my way, on my own and falling short for His ways of gentle success
I laid all my baggage at His feet, my addiction, illnesses and all my pain, sorrow, fear and worry at His feet.

If someone approaches you with one of these comments, it is an offer to welcome you to ask questions, to have a deep conversation about your walk with the Lord.

I say, "I am healed because of Jesus. I welcome Him to my life to teach me and love me. I am no longer an orphan. I have a new identity as the son or daughter of God, the brother of Jesus and to become the vessel of God's Spirit and the family of believers are my kin."

When you have a personal experience with the Trinity, God, Jesus and Holy Spirit write it down. Find someone, a believer to talk to about it. I have hundreds of thousands of experiences with the Trinity. So, I will explain that just as you are one person, you have mind, spirit and body, that worked together to make you. This is the simple correlation. The Trinity, God, Jesus and Holy Spirit are all one God but different parts the persons of the God head.

God the all and all, Jesus became man, "*the body*", Spirit is within you and guiding you. The Holy Spirit is a part of God that was sent to you, after you welcome Jesus, "*the Savior*", into your life. He sent Holy Spirit to help you, teach you, comfort you and show you Jesus' perfect peace.

Have you ever seen some tender eyes? Those eyes have compassion, love and peace even in the toughest of times. Those eyes are called "Jesus Eyes." You can tell a sister or brother in Jesus Christ by their eyes. By their ability to know, or see, or feel or hear God. God, the Creator, always wanted an awesome relationship with His creations. Adam His first creation messed it up, was treasonous to the authority of God. Jesus came to fix that mess. On Easter we celebrate the restored relationship with God, because of Jesus Christ's sacrifice.

Of course, Christians have fancy names for all these things. We call it Christianese (or Christianize), a way of explaining a concept in one quick word. Like, the golden chain of salvation, or a bible reference like Romans 8:8, or Romans 8 The Passion Translation (TPT). This is for later when you join a group or a mentor comes along or even a church helps you understand more deeply the true depths of God's love for you.

Don't get caught up in the complexity. God simply loves you. Welcome Jesus to your heart and to give Him your baggage. Find a person with Jesus' eyes to help you. Be Blessed!

Am I Really a Christian?

$\mathcal{M}$any people are in the habit of categorizing everything. God is not. Am I a Christian if I am not Catholic? I was Catholic am I now not Christian? I am a protestant am I saved? I was in a cult. Will God hold that against me?

Oh, the endless questions I have received from total strangers about the possibility of getting to heaven man's way.

You want to know, am I in the book of life? Am I saved? Ask yourself.

- Have I accepted that Jesus loves me and I love Him?
- Have I with my will and my mouth invited Him into my life; to talk to and have Him talk to me?
- Have I humbled myself and surrendered to the point I have asked Him for His forgiveness for the known and unknown sins of my past.

In the bible, Book of Romans is the easiest of hundreds of places God welcomes you. When reading the bible, it is often hard to understand who, is the I. This is the best place to answer your question. The *italic* will be my comments to help.

Romans 10:1-13 NIV

Brothers and sisters, my (*Paul the writer*) heart's desire and prayer to God for the Israelites is that they may be saved.

2 For I (*Paul the writer*) can testify about them that they are zealous for God, but their zeal is not based on knowledge. *(a personal experience with the Creator is the key to understanding His love)*

3 Since they *(the Israelites and Gentiles ... perhaps you)* did not know the righteousness of God and sought to establish their own, they did not submit to God's righteousness. *(Obedience is important)*

4 Christ is the culmination of the law so that there may be righteousness for everyone who believes. *(EVERYONE)*

5 Moses writes this about the righteousness that is by the law: "The person who does these things will live by them." *(It is said that the letter of the law takes you to your knees to pray and seek God's help. Then Christ Jesus comes and gives you His hand and picks you up to show you His love and sacrifice to take you into a new world of righteousness, undeserved but freely given. That way you are free from the slavery to sin. And become an adopted son or daughter of the Creator.)*

6 But the righteousness that is by faith says: "Do not say in your heart, 'Who will ascend into heaven?'" (that is, to bring Christ down)

7 "or 'Who will descend into the deep?'" (that is, to bring Christ up from the dead).

8 But what does it say? "The word is near you; *(Christ Jesus is the WORD)* it is in your mouth and in your heart," that is, the message concerning faith that we proclaim:

9 If you declare with your mouth, "Jesus is Lord," and believe in your heart that God raised him from the dead, you will be saved.

10 For it is with your heart that you believe and are justified, and it is with your mouth that you profess your faith and are saved.

11 As Scripture says, "**Anyone who believes in him will never be put to shame**."

12 For there is no difference between Jew and Gentile—the same Lord is Lord of all and richly blesses all who call on him, 13 for, "**Everyone who calls on the name of the Lord will be saved.**

Mary's Comments:

It does not say if you stand on your head and clap three times. It is done! The word of God did it all. Just receive! God loves unity. We are united in the love of Jesus and in our praise and worship. All else are barriers to unity. Welcome to the family.

CONCLUSION

I anticipate this book has been an encouragement to you and your life's walk. There is so much good in the world and it is just waiting for you to breakthrough and see it. Freedom like earth has never known is yours to receive with all the authority that God is releasing to us now.

It may look very dark as I write this, but even in the storm you see the light. You see the drastic flip on the horizon. Celebrate the new future before it fully arrives because it is here.

Praise God with unbridled worship, as it should be! Live in His unending love. May God bless you abundantly.

I want to pray for each reader, this is my prayer.

Dear Papa Father God,

Please let all who have eyes to see and ears to hear be filled by Your love, I personally know and have tried to put into this book for them to receive. Please deliver them from the ills of this time. Make their path up the new era mountains smooth and filled with the joy of You. Show them how to receive all You wish to share with them.

I wish to see them all in heaven. Help them see a way to teach the youth how to never have this evil take hold of our exquisite planet again. Break off all ungodly soul ties and generational curses. Help them see the totality of Your Jesus' sacrifice. Release them from any ungodly spirit. Heal them in body soul and spirit. Lavish Your love on them. Give them all your generational blessings.

I declare that Your will is being completed now. That the nations and their people will be delivered and the world will be free. That the gospel will be spread throughout the whole world and the goats and the sheep will be sorted. We will see the Psalm 91 deliverance and the Psalm 92 freedom, and the defeat of our enemies occur in our days. That the Greatest Ever Revival and its abundant harvest has started and will be fruitful.

I decree it is finish.

Praise the Lord for His endless mercies and love. Praise God for these amazing feats that no man can take credit for. Praise God for the great move of His Spirit and His angel armies. Praise God for the upgrade of His children's authority.

Amen and Amen.

ABOUT THE AUTHOR
AND ARTIST

Mary Leonard, Wife, Mother, Artist, Author, Prophetic, Preacher, Spiritual Coach and Teacher. Mary has been communicating with Papa Father God since early childhood. God, Jesus and Holy Spirit have been talking to Mary about this time we are in for many years. She has spoken on this subject in churches and civic groups. She was compelled to write this book to give you a look into the bright and beautiful future God has been planning since before time. The most recent discussions are exhilarating. Celebrate! We are on the threshold of a major miracle. You were born for a time such as this.

Mary has been painting the "Mariahsachin Style Art" for half a century. The paintings are an unusually simple, still profoundly complex, abstraction of the unknown yet known. She is grateful for her deeper growth through Mariahsachin, painting with the Holy Spirit. She paints spiritual awareness in her paintings from chaos to order.

Mary's other books include *God's Little Princess, The God Factor in Recovery, Mariahsachin.*

ABOUT THE BOOK

This book is a long prophetic word. It is a prophecy to give you a look into the bright and beautiful future God has been planning since before time. He has been talking to Mary about this time we are in, for many years. The most recent discussions are exhilarating. Celebrate! We are on the threshold of a major miracle. You were born for a time such as this. How are you seeing your new future in the "New Era Mountains?"

Change is here. It is your time to shine. This is an encouraging clearly written book with steps to take to change your life forever. Speak life into your life. Mary gives examples of hearing, seeing, knowing and feeling God, so you can do it also. This book includes the new names of the New Era Mountains and how they are drastically changing for the good.

Mary has decided to get this book out fast, using a more casual style of writing and editing. This book is for your knowledge and not for a writing class. Hopefully the love for you and humanity will override any imperfections in the technical aspects of its editing.

One recent sentence about the evil in this world, God said, "I am going to turn them on their heads, upside down, inside out and DONE!" This is a Passover of His children and a judgement of all the evil around the world. Praise God!

Internet Presence

Websites: www.2mea.com

Email: info@2mea.com subject line put something like ... comment, request, edits, questions and so on.

Rumble.com Channels – Mariahsachin or Painting in the Spirit

List of Painting Styles

Co-founder of Mariahsachin Painting Style, 1969

List of Books

God's Little Princess, A Child's Abstract Journey

Mariahsachin, Painting Style

The God Factor in Recovery, Mess to Miracle

List of Songs

Let Freedom Ring in all the Earth

List of Paintings in this book are from:
Mary Leonard's Testimonies Collection
All 36" by 36"

Authority – Oil	Sweeping – Oil and Acrylic
Horn – Acrylic	Battle for Freedom – Oil
Revival – Oil and Acrylic	Trumpets – Oil and Acrylic
Guardians – Oil and Acrylic	Happy Little Clouds – Oil